SUPREME DAMAGE

Rescuing Representative Government from Judicial Overreach

SUPREME DAMAGE

Rescuing Representative Government from Judicial Overreach

Thurman Leonard Smith

Smithurmann Publishing
Winchester Massachusetts
781-729-3832

ISBN 978-1-7335095-2-7
Library of Congress Control Number 2019914210

Dedicated to all lovers of liberty and defenders of the Constitution

Foreword

The outrageous overreach of the courts has long bothered me. But especially disturbing was the 2015 Supreme Court decision that invalidated a state law—that was within the state's power to enact—providing that marriage was an institution for one man and one woman, finding it was no longer binding and that any two people had a right to marry, even if they were of the same sex. It was chilling to think that the people, as represented in Congress and by state legislators, are no longer in charge of their governments. Instead, over the decades, much power has been assumed by a handful of unelected lawyers in a black robe who are not politically accountable to the people. This revision of process is not what a representative republic is all about.

In this book, eighteen erroneously decided cases are described in thirteen chapters. The reader will find the background story, the arguments of both sides, where the Court erred, the consequences of the ruling, and suggested solutions. At the end of each chapter are suggestions for further reading and, where appropriate, action.

The Afterword briefly describes other poorly decided cases that are not covered in the main text. An appendix defines some terms commonly used in adjudication. For reference, the Constitution and its first fourteen amendments are presented in the last appendix.

Links to related web resources appear in context. The links

are not essential for understanding the content but could add much depth. E-book readers should click anywhere in the URL. To return to the text, click on the tab for the book at the top of your reader. All the URLs have an ID, such as W1-AA. A roster of URLs with their ID is available at

http://www.smithurman.com/sdlinks.htm.

This site is where print readers with an internet-connected device handy can easily link to the websites while reading. Search for the ID as shown in the book, then click on the URL to its right.

I defend new word creation if it is etymologically plausible. One in this tome is "malaffect," which is not in any dictionary but should be! Its meaning is obvious.

In this effort, I was aided by author and political maven Michael Isenberg (*Full Asylum* and *The Thread of Reason* (MonteFerropress.com)), whose comments made for valuable improvements in content and organization, by author and activist Amy Contrada, who made substantial enhancements to the chapter on *Lawrence v. Texas* and *Obergefell v. Hodges* and by attorney-editor Liz Seif (inawordediting.com) for a very constructive final review.

Thurman Leonard Smith
Winchester, Massachusetts
June 15, 2020

Introduction

What are the Supreme Court's powers?

"The judiciary, from the nature of its functions, will always be the least dangerous to the political rights of the Constitution."
— Alexander Hamilton in *Federalist No. 78*

WI-AA http://www.constitution.org/fed/federa78.htm

If only Hamilton had been proven right! Unfortunately, over the decades, particularly since the late nineteenth century, federal courts, including especially the Supreme Court, have taken on a role in making public policy to the degree that many believe the judiciary has become the most dangerous branch. Whole categories of life previously reserved for the legislative process at either the federal or state level have been reordered by Court rulings. With the stakes having so steeply risen, each new vacancy in the Supreme Court results in a knock-down, drag-out brawl over who will fill it. Thus, the dubious ad hominem charges against Clarence Thomas (1991) and Brett Kavanaugh (2019) in their Senate confirmation hearings.

Judicial activism

The primary concern of those who believe that the Court has become a danger to representative government, the federal structure, and ordered liberty arises when the Court engages in what has come to be called "judicial activism," which is manifested in nine varieties:

abusing precedent, contorting text, importing foreign law, exhibiting judicial dishonesty, interjecting judicial imperialism, applying "living constitutionalism," nullifying rights, playing favorites, and playing legislator.

The three that are most at play in the cases in these chapters are living constitutionalism, playing legislator, and nullifying rights. Living constitutionalism is the view that judges can construe the Constitution to fit new needs and conditions that were not foreseen by the original drafters without regard to the text of the Constitution, the meaning of its words, or the intent of its authors. Much mischief has occurred because of this notion. Justice Breyer has been a keen proponent of this approach.

Sadly, there has not been an effective way to correct an errant Court, but in our journey, some solutions are suggested in the form of Constitutional amendments.

Some history

There is good reason to believe that the Framers of the Constitution did not see the Court as having a policy role. Madison's August 15, 1787 notes on the Convention show that a proposal to submit all acts of Congress to both the Executive and the Supreme Court for review was rejected by the Convention.

WI-AB http://www.nhccs.org/dfc-0815.txt

In *Federalist 78*, Hamilton also allowed that the "interpretation of the laws is the proper and peculiar province of the courts. . . . It therefore belongs to them to ascertain its meaning, as well as the meaning of any particular act proceeding from the legislative body." That expression would seem to anticipate that the Court could at least comment that a law conflicted with the Constitution and perhaps overrule it. Indeed, critics of this meaning of "judicial review" were at a loss to explain what other mechanism there was to protect people from laws that violated the natural rights guaranteed in the Constitution.

If the power of the Court to overturn legislation was unclear in the early days of the republic, it was firmly established in *Marbury v. Madison* (1803). Not long after this decision, a common understanding developed that it fell to the Supreme Court to determine what the Constitution says. From there, it is held that the Court has the power to determine the limitations placed on the two other branches of the federal government as well as the states.

Having lost the 1800 election, John Adams hurried to make last-minute appointments of fellow Federalists to various offices. Not all of his writs were able to be served before Jefferson's inauguration, including that for William Marbury as justice of the peace for the new District of Columbia. So Marbury filed a suit seeking to have the Supreme Court, rather than an inferior court, perform the task of issuing the writ, based on the 1789 Judiciary Act, which gave the Court original jurisdiction in situations not specified in the Constitution. The Court, while acceding that Marbury should have gotten his commission, correctly declined to issue the writ because its justices gave deference to the Constitution, the highest written law.

Chief Justice John Marshall's decision affirmed the need for Constitutional review by the judiciary, but not judicial supremacy. That would be a coequal power of courts to judge acts of the other branches as to their conformance with the Constitution and to refuse to apply judicial concurrence to enable laws contradicting the Constitution.

But a full and nuanced reading of this decision could yield conclusions other than the doctrine of "judicial review" as practiced post-Marbury. An excellent analysis along these lines can be found in a 2004 paper, "The Irrepressible Myth of Marbury," by Michael Stokes Paulsen, chairman at the University of St. Thomas School of Law (Minneapolis, Minnesota):

WI-AC https://repository.law.umich.edu/mlr/vol101/iss8/7

Those dangerous footnotes

Sometimes the damage that the Supreme Court does lies in the obiter dicta (Latin for "by the way") commentary in a footnote to an opinion. These comments are not part of the formal ruling, but they can influence decisions in later cases.

The first serious case was *United States v. Butler* (1936), where in the body of the opinion were comments that pointed to a new expansive interpretation of taxing for the "general welfare" and separated what the federal government could spend for as enumerated in the Constitution. From then on, it was open season for new spending not related to one of the tasks and powers given to the federal government.

There soon followed the famous footnote four in *United States v. Carolene Products* (1938), which encouraged courts to assume that economic legislation was constitutional unless it conflicted with specific prohibitions in the Constitution or affected certain minorities. The language of footnote four launched a new role for the federal courts. That a law might interfere with a natural right, such as engaging in an activity to earn a living, was thereafter not so easily nixed.

And in *Plyler v. Doe* (1982), commentary in the footnotes by Justice William Brennan led to an acceptance of the idea that most anyone who happened to be born in the United States was automatically a citizen, regardless of parentage.

For further reading

Original Intent: The Courts, the Constitution, and Religion by David Barton; 1996, Wall Builders

WI-AD https://shop.wallbuilders.com/original-intent-paperback

The Supremacists: The Tyranny of Judges and How to Stop It by Phyllis Schlafly; 2004, Spence Publishing Company

WI-AE https://www.goodreads.com/book/show/598468.The_Supremacists

Men in Black by Mark Levin; 2005, Regnery

WI-AF https://www.goodreads.com/book/show/569404.Men_in_Black

The Dirty Dozen: How Twelve Supreme Court Cases Radically Expanded Government and Eroded Freedom by Robert Levy & William Mellor; 2009, Cato Institute

WI-AG https://www.cato.org/events/dirty-dozen-are-they-worst-supreme-court-cases-modern-era

Terms of Engagement: How Our Courts Should Enforce the Constitution's Promise of Limited Government by Clark M. Neily; 2013, Encounter Books

WI-AH https://www.encounterbooks.com/books/terms-of-engagement-how-our-courts-should-enforce-the-constitutions-promise-of-limited-government/

Stolen Sovereignty: How to Stop Unelected Judges from Transforming America by Daniel Horowitz; 2016, WND Books

WI-AI https://www.conservativereview.com/news/10-takeaways-from-stolen-sovereignty/

The Most Dangerous Branch: Inside the Supreme Court's Assault on the Constitution by David Kaplan; 2018, Crown Publishing (Random House)

WI-AJ http://davidakaplan.com/books/the-most-dangerous-branch-hc

1~*United States v. Wong Kim Ark* (1898) and *Plyler v. Doe* (1982)

It's not the physical location of birth that defines citizenship, but whether your parents are citizens, and the express or implied consent to the jurisdiction of the sovereign.—Phyllis Schlafly

In 1898, the Supreme Court issued a decision that substantially changed the meaning and purpose of the citizenship clause of the Fourteenth Amendment as it had been construed before this case. The decision led to a consequential reduction of control over immigration and adverse effects on civil society and government services. Eighty-four years later, a footnote in a ruling was construed by courts and immigration officials to mean that even children born to parents in the country illegally are to be considered citizens.

In *United States v. Wong Kim Ark*, the Supreme Court ruled that a person who is born in the United States of parents who, at the time of his birth, are subjects of a foreign power, who have a permanent domicile and residence in the United States, and who are here to carry on a business and are not employed in any diplomatic or official capacity by the foreign power to which they are subject, becomes, at the time of his birth, a citizen of the United States by virtue of the first clause of the Fourteenth Amendment.

Before the case

This case highlighted disagreements over the precise meaning of one phrase in the citizenship clause; that is, the provision that a person born in the United States who is "subject to the jurisdiction thereof" acquires automatic citizenship. The Court's majority concluded that this phrase did not mean only being required to obey U.S. law while in the United States; but interpreted it in a way that granted U.S. citizenship to almost all children born on American soil (a concept known as *jus soli*). The dissenters, more accurately, argued that "subject to the jurisdiction of" meant not being subject to any foreign power; that is, not being claimed as a citizen by another country via *jus sanguinis* (inheriting citizenship from a parent). This interpretation, in the minority's view, would have excluded "the children of foreigners, happening to be born to them while passing through the country."

Until after the Civil War, there was no definition of citizenship in U.S. law, but it was widely accepted that anyone born in the United States was automatically a citizen. This application of birthplace citizenship via inherited English common law was upheld in an 1844 New York state case, *Lynch v. Clarke*. The court held that a woman born in New York City of alien parents temporarily traveling there was a U.S. citizen. In an era when travel to a country not surrounded by numerous other countries was difficult and when generous welfare and access to public services was not an attraction, that lenient practice did not present much threat of unwanted invasions of persons not cleared for immigration and an organized path to citizenship.

Post–Civil War

After the Civil War and the subsequent abolition of slavery, Congress enacted the Civil Rights Act of 1866. One provision of this law declared as citizens not only the freed slaves but "all persons born in the United States and not subject to any foreign power, excluding Indians not taxed."

Concerns were raised that the citizenship guarantee in the Civil Rights Act might be repealed by a later Congress or struck down as unconstitutional by the courts. So, soon after its passage, Congress drafted the Fourteenth Amendment. Among its provisions was a clause that assured a guarantee of citizenship in the Constitution by stating, "All persons born or naturalized in the United States, and subject to the jurisdiction thereof, are citizens of the United States and the State wherein they reside."

Senator Jacob Howard of Michigan proposed the citizenship clause in May 1866 as an amendment to a joint resolution from the House of Representatives, which had framed the proposed amendment's initial draft. The debate on the proposed new language in the Senate focused on whether Howard's language would apply more broadly than the wording of the 1866 Civil Rights Act.

Howard said that the clause "is simply declaratory of what I regard as the law of the land already, that every person born within the limits of the United States, and subject to their jurisdiction, is by virtue of natural law and national law a citizen of the United States." He added that citizenship "will not, of course, include persons born in the United States who are foreigners, aliens, who belong to the families of ambassadors or foreign ministers accredited to the Government of the United

States."

Enter the Fourteenth Amendment

Upon its return to the House, the proposed Fourteenth Amendment prompted little debate, and no one spoke in opposition to the Senate's addition of the citizenship clause. The complete proposed amendment was approved by the House in June 1866 and was ratified two years later.

After its adoption and before *Wong Kim Ark*, the question of birthplace citizenship for children of aliens arose only regarding American Indians and Chinese. The issue of whether the citizenship clause applied to persons born to Chinese immigrants in the United States appeared before federal courts first in an 1884 case (*Elk v. Wilkins*) and later in an 1892 case (*Gee Fook Sing v. United States*). Both were claims on reentry to the United States by men born in the United States of Chinese parents. Both cases were decided in favor of the claim of citizenship on the basis of having been born in the United States. These cases were never appealed to the Supreme Court but may have established a precedent for *United States v. Wong Kim Ark.*

Pre-*Wong* views of the citizenship clause show its limited purpose

Until *Wong,* the Court had never ruled that the meaning of the Fourteenth Amendment was to grant citizenship to everyone who happened to be born in the United States. Some examples:

Supreme Court opinion in the *Slaughterhouse Cases* (1873), in which the majority noted in passing that

> the phrase "subject to the jurisdiction thereof" was

> intended to exclude from its operation children of [foreign] ministers, consuls, and citizens or subjects of foreign states born within the United States.

Are not illegal aliens still subjects of the country they fled?

Supreme Court opinion in *Ex Parte Virginia* (1879):

> [The Fourteenth Amendment was] primarily designed to give freedom to persons of the African race, prevent their future enslavement, make them citizens, prevent discriminating State legislation against their rights as freemen, and secure to them the ballot.

Supreme Court opinion in *Strauder v. West Virginia* (1880):

> The Fourteenth Amendment was framed and adopted to assure to the colored race the enjoyment of all the civil rights that, under the law, are enjoyed by white persons, and to give to that race the protection of the general government in that enjoyment whenever it should be denied by the States.

Supreme Court opinion in *Elk v. Wilkins* (1884):

> The main object of the opening sentence of the Fourteenth Amendment was to put it beyond doubt that all persons, white or black, and whether formerly slaves or not, born or naturalized in the United States, and owing no allegiance to any alien power, should be citizens of the United States. The evident meaning of (the words, "and subject to the jurisdiction thereof") is, not merely subject in some respect or degree to the jurisdiction of the United States, but entirely subject to their political

> jurisdiction, and owing them direct and immediate allegiance. Persons not thus subject to the jurisdiction of the United States at the time of birth cannot become so afterward, except by being naturalized.

The case

Wong Kim Ark was born in San Francisco to Chinese parents around 1871. He worked mostly as a cook. His parents returned to China in 1888, but Wong remained in California. Wong visited his parents in 1890, and upon his return to the United States he was readmitted without incident. In November 1894, Wong sailed again to China for another visit, but when he returned the next year the Collector of Customs at the Port of San Francisco denied him permission to enter the country. He argued that Wong was not a U.S. citizen even though he was born in the United States and that because his parents were Chinese he was instead a Chinese subject.

The U.S. District Court for Northern California rules for Wong

The arguments presented in the federal district court centered around which interpretation of the phrase "subject to the jurisdiction thereof" in the citizenship clause should govern a situation involving a child born in the United States to foreign parents. Wong's attorneys argued that the phrase meant "subject to the laws of the United States." That is the requirement that aliens owe in a foreign country to obey its laws. This interpretation, based on English common law, would encompass virtually everyone born in the United States via the principle of citizenship based on place of birth.

The U.S. government claimed that "subject to the jurisdiction thereof" meant "to be subject to the political jurisdiction of the United States," an interpretation based on international law that would exclude parents and their children who owed allegiance to another country via the idea that citizenship is inherited from a parent.

Up to this time, the question of the citizenship status of U.S.-born children of alien parents had never been decided by the Supreme Court. The U.S. government argued that Wong's claim to U.S. citizenship was ruled out by the Supreme Court's interpretation of jurisdiction in its 1873 *Slaughterhouse Cases* ruling. But the district court judge concluded that the language in question was obiter dictum and not directly relevant to the *Wong* case.

Wong's attorneys cited an 1884 case out of the same court that conveyed citizenship in a similar situation. The district court judge agreed that that case definitively settled the question of citizenship for Wong and others like him, as far as federal courts in the Ninth Circuit were concerned, given the absence of clear direction from the Supreme Court. The judge noted that another part of the Supreme Court's *Slaughterhouse Cases* opinion said that "it is only necessary that [a man] should be born or naturalized in the United States to be a citizen of the Union." So, the district court ruled that "subject to the jurisdiction thereof" referred to being subject to U.S. law (the first of the two proposed interpretations) and declared Wong Kim Ark to be a citizen because he was born in the United States.

The Supreme Court rules for Wong

The U.S. government appealed the district court ruling

directly to the Supreme Court. Oral arguments were held in March of 1897. The Court considered the central question in the case to be "whether a child born in the United States, of parents of Chinese descent, who, at the time of his birth, are subjects of the Emperor of China, but have a permanent domicile and residence in the United States, and are there carrying on business, and are not employed in any diplomatic or official capacity under the Emperor of China, becomes at the time of his birth a citizen of the United States" via the Fourteenth Amendment.

The decision

In March of 1898, the Supreme Court held, 6–2, that Wong Kim Ark had acquired U.S. citizenship at birth and that "the American citizenship which Wong Kim Ark acquired by birth within the United States has not been lost or taken away by anything happening since his birth."

The Court held that the citizenship clause needed to be interpreted in light of English common law, which had included as subjects virtually all native-born children, excluding only those who were born to foreign rulers or diplomats, born on alien public ships, or born to enemy forces engaged in hostile occupation of the country's territory. The majority held that the subject-to-the-jurisdiction phrase excluded from U.S. citizenship only those persons covered by one of these three exceptions. It concluded that none of these three exceptions to U.S. citizenship applied to Wong; in particular, it observed that "during all the time of their said residence in the United States, as domiciled residents therein, the said mother and father of said Wong Kim Ark were engaged in the operation of a business, and were never engaged in any diplomatic or official capacity under the emperor of China."

Dissents

Chief Justice Melville Fuller was joined by Associate Justice John Harlan in a dissent that was predicated upon the recognition of the international law doctrine. The dissenters argued that after independence, the history of U.S. citizenship law had broken with English common law tradition and that the principle of a child inheriting his or her father's citizenship by descent regardless of birthplace had been more pervasive in U.S. legal history. The dissenters claimed, based on an assessment of U.S. and Chinese treaty and naturalization law, that "the children of Chinese born in this country do not, *ipso facto*, become citizens of the United States unless the fourteenth amendment overrides both treaty and statute."

The dissenters further argued that "it is not open to reasonable doubt that the words 'subject to the jurisdiction thereof,' in the amendment, were used as synonymous with the words 'and not subject to any foreign power.'" In the dissenters' view, excessive reliance on birthplace as the principal determinant of citizenship would lead to a condition in which "the children of foreigners, happening to be born to them while passing through the country, whether of royal parentage or not, or whether of the Mongolian, Malay or other race, were eligible to the presidency, while children of our citizens, born abroad, were not."

After the case

However flawed, the parameters of the *jus soli* principle, as set out by the court in this case, have never since been seriously questioned by the Supreme Court and have been accepted as settled law by lower courts.

In 1942 an unsuccessful effort was made by the Native Sons of the Golden West to convince the Supreme Court to revisit and overrule *Wong Kim Ark* in a case (*Regan v. King*) challenging the citizenship status of roughly 2,600 U.S.-born persons of Japanese parents.

Since the 1990s, controversy has arisen over the prevailing practice of granting automatic citizenship to U.S.-born children of illegal immigrants. And legal scholars disagree over whether the *Wong Kim Ark* precedent applies when alien parents are in the country illegally. From time to time in Congress, attempts have been made to restrict birthright citizenship, either via statutory redefinition of the term "jurisdiction" or by overriding both the *Wong* ruling and the citizenship clause itself through a constitutional amendment, but no such proposal has been successful.

A 2010 review by University of Baltimore law professor Garrett Epps of the history of the citizenship clause noted that *Wong Kim Ark* held that the guarantee of birthright citizenship "applies to children of foreigners present on American soil" and states that the Supreme Court "has not re-examined this issue since the concept of 'illegal alien' entered the language."

W1-AA
http://digitalcommons.wcl.american.edu/aulr/vol60/iss2/2/

Enter *Plyler v. Doe* and anchor babies

While *Wong Kim Ark* could be defended as a ruling based on common law, it became a wedge for unintended paths to citizenship. In several Supreme Court decisions affirming the citizenship of U.S.-born individuals of Chinese or Japanese parents, the Court has affirmed birthplace as the primary determinant of U.S. citizenship. The Court's holding that the language of the Constitution should be understood in light of the common law has been cited in numerous Supreme Court decisions. The *Wong* Court's understanding of Fourteenth Amendment jurisdiction was cited in *Plyler v. Doe,* a 1982 case involving the rights of illegal immigrants to state-funded education.

Education: who's in charge?

The Texas Education Agency said that illegal immigrants are not entitled to free public education, but Justice Brennan manufactured this novel entitlement in his opinion for the 5–4 majority. As one might imagine, *Plyler* has wreaked havoc on public education and school finances ever since.

The reasoning the Court gave for overturning a reasonable state law was that the equal protection clause of the Fourteenth Amendment guaranteed the equal protection of the laws to illegal aliens, requiring Americans to school these children for free—even though such persons were not really in the state's jurisdiction as they weren't supposed to be there in the first place! And even if one believes that the Fourteenth Amendment incorporates all of the amendments in the Bill of Rights, making them applicable to the states as well as the federal government, the equal protection clause should not extend to discretionary benefits offered by a state. Additionally, the ruling never considered the harm done to American parents and children. As parents labor to pay ever-higher taxes, their children must share their schools with scores of illegal aliens—most not English-speaking unless they take on the double burden of private schools.

The fatal footnote

Sometimes the damage done by the Supreme Court lies in the *obiter dicta* in an opinion, sometimes in a footnote. Even though these comments are not part of the ruling, the views in them often find their way into later decisions.

Such is the case with this decision, where the real damage came in a footnote slipped into the opinion. Brennan's remarks included the dubious statement that "no plausible distinction with respect to Fourteenth Amendment 'jurisdiction' can be drawn between resident aliens whose entry into the United States was lawful and resident aliens whose entry was unlawful."

Brennan's authority for this comment was an opinion in a 1912 treatise written by an obscure Washington lawyer, Clement Bouvé. So, on one hand, we have over a century with the Fourteenth Amendment not conferring citizenship on children born to illegal immigrants. Then, suddenly, we have a remark in a book by an unremarkable D.C. lawyer that was referred to in a footnote in a 1982 opinion, and the whole immigration regime changes.

There are, of course, a host of "plausible distinction[s]." Among them: legal immigrants have been checked for contagious diseases and subversive ties and have some qualifications to be here other than just happening to have sneaked across the border. Alas, ever since *Plyler*, the federal government has acted as if birthright citizenship was the law of the land all along. A truly harmful case of judges making law, even if inadvertently! This 2010 *Human Events* article by author Ann Coulter summarizes the damage:

W1-AB https://humanevents.com/2010/08/04/justice-brennans-footnote-gave-us-anchor-babies

Resistance commences

In 2013, a federal appellate decision (*Oforji v. Ashcroft*) criticized the *jus soli* holding in *Wong* in connection with illegal immigration but at the same time conceded that the courts were powerless to change this rule and urged Congress to do so.

Some legal scholars opposed to the idea that *jus soli* should apply to the children of undocumented immigrants have argued that the *Wong* precedent does not apply when alien parents are in the country illegally. One is John C. Eastman, a former dean of the Chapman University School of Law, who has argued that *Wong Kim Ark* does not entitle U.S.-born children of undocumented immigrants to automatic citizenship because being subject to the jurisdiction of the United States refers to "full and complete jurisdiction," which does not apply to aliens who are in the country illegally. "Justice Gray failed to appreciate what he seemed to have understood in *Elk v. Wilkins*: that there is a difference between territorial jurisdiction and the more complete, allegiance-obliging jurisdiction that the Fourteenth Amendment codified."

Eastman further argued that *Wong Kim Ark* was fundamentally flawed in the way the ruling dealt with the concept of jurisdiction and that the Indian Citizenship Act of 1924, which followed *Wong Kim Ark*, would not have been necessary if Congress had believed

> that the citizenship clause confers citizenship merely by accident of birth. Indeed, Congress has by its own actions with respect to Native

> Americans both before and after this Court's decision in *Wong* rejected the claim that the citizenship clause itself confers citizenship merely by accident of birth. None of these citizenship acts would have been necessary; indeed, all would have been redundant under the expansive view of the citizenship clause propounded by Justice Gray.

Eastman's full article can be found at:

W1-AC https://www.heritage.org/the-constitution/report/feudalism-consent-rethinking-birthright-citizenship

Professor of law Lino Graglia of the University of Texas argued that even if *Wong Kim Ark* settled the status of children of legal residents, it did not do so for children of illegal residents. Graglia maintained that the case weighs against automatic birthright for illegal immigrants because the Court denied such citizenship for a similar group, namely "children of alien enemies, born during and within their hostile occupation." His analysis is at this CNSnews site:

W1-AD http://www.cnsnews.com/commentary/lino-graglia/birthright-citizenship-not-merely-unreasonable-and-harmful-irrational-and

Charles Wood, former counsel to the Senate Judiciary Committee's subcommittee on immigration, has also opposed the practice. He urged in 1999 that it be stopped as quickly as possible, either by a constitutional amendment or an act of Congress:

> The needed reforms should be completed expeditiously. . . . [I]n every week that

> passes thousands more children of illegal aliens are born in this country, and each is now granted citizenship. If these reforms are not accomplished one way or another soon, "We the People of the United States" risk losing control of the nation's future.

W1-AE
http://www.thesocialcontract.com/artman2/publish/tsc1503/article_1320.shtml

Anchor-baby impact

It is bad enough that the federal government has not actively fought illegal immigration in the George W. Bush–Obama period. But the added consequences of birthright citizenship via *Wong* and *Plyler* have hugely compounded the problem. This issue is also commonly termed the "anchor baby" problem. This term describes a concern that is related to and complicates the administration of our immigration law because our immigration admission criteria are based so heavily on family relationships, and U.S. citizens may sponsor extended family members for legal immigration status. "Anchor baby" children may instantly qualify for welfare and other state and local benefit programs. Additionally, with the passage of the 1965 Immigration and Nationality Act, the child may sponsor other family members for entry into the United States when he or she reaches the age of twenty-one to effect "chain migration."

Not unexpectedly, the impact, both economic and social, of the unexpected and uninvited new "citizens" is not small. In 2016 the Pew Research Center issued a paper that outlined some of the adverse consequences, as summarized in this *New*

American column:

W1-AF https://www.thenewamerican.com/usnews/immigration/item/24518-new-pew-report-significant-economic-impact-of-illegals-anchor-babies

In late 2017, *Breitbart* reported that the number of United-States–born children who were given birthright citizenship despite at least one of their parents being an illegal alien living in the country outnumbered one year of all U.S. births.

W1-AG https://www.breitbart.com/big-government/2017/12/28/anchor-baby-population-in-u-s-exceeds-one-year-of-american-births/

One attraction of entering the United States to give birth is our modern welfare state, which creates pervasive incentives for immigrants, especially when they have children here. When they and their newly minted "citizen" children stay, there are increased costs to taxpayers for public services, especially as many such families are in income brackets that qualify for various levels of assistance. A summary of the scope of the public costs of children born to illegal immigrants is found in an article by Ian Tuttle in the August 21, 2015, *National Review*.

W1-AH http://www.nationalreview.com/article/422921/birthright-citizenship-economic-costs-incentives

The spread of birth tourism

Radio and TV reports have reported on a growing trend, especially among Chinese visitors to the United States—using "birth hotels" to secure U.S. citizenship for their child and leave open the possibility of future immigration by the parents to the

United States.

National Public Radio: "Foreigners Visiting 'Birth Hotels' in California Draw Local Ire" by Audie Cornish, January 4, 2013:

W1-AI http://www.npr.org/2013/01/04/168642107/foreigners-visiting-birth-hotels-in-california-draw-local-ire

ABC News: "Chinese Women Pay to Give Birth at California Maternity Mansion, Secure Citizenship for Babies" by Alyssa Newcomb, December 2, 2012:

W1-AJ https://abcnews.go.com/US/chinese-women-pay-give-birth-california-maternity-mansion/story?id=17862251

In a 2015 study, the Center for Immigration Studies estimates that 36,000 babies are born to "birth tourists" annually.

W1-AK http://cis.org/camarota/there-are-possibly-36000-birth-tourists-annually

Huffington Post China correspondent Matt Sheehan wrote in 2015 that pregnant Chinese women typically spend around $20,000 to stay in the facilities during their final months of pregnancy and an additional month to recuperate and await their new baby's U.S. passport:

W1-AL http://www.huffingtonpost.com/2015/05/01/china-us-birth-tourism_n_7187180.html

More recently, pregnant Chinese women have been choosing to travel and give birth in Saipan, a U.S. territory in the Pacific, for the same purpose, as reported in this 2016 *Saipan Tribune* article:

W1-AM https://www.saipantribune.com/index.php/birth-foreign-parents-skyrockets/

Center for Immigration Studies Director Mark Krikorian

examined the impact of birth tourism in this 2018 Fox News interview:

W1-AN https://cis.org/Mark-Krikorian-Discusses-Birth-Tourism

No constructive response as yet

The original intent of the Fourteenth Amendment was clearly not to facilitate illegal aliens defying U.S. law and obtaining citizenship for their offspring or obtaining benefits at taxpayer expense. The United States is unusual in its offer to extend citizenship to anyone born on its soil. Among other countries, only Canada has such a policy. But since 2014 there has been increasing agitation to end this lax policy as it was encouraging Chinese women to enter the country in the ninth month of pregnancy. As the law now stands (subsection 3(2) of the Citizenship Act), Canadian citizenship is not granted to a child born in Canada if neither parent is a Canadian citizen or permanent resident.

Because this misapplication of the Fourteenth Amendment has not been corrected, the funds that state and local governments must provide to anchor babies amount to a virtual tax on U.S. citizens to subsidize illegal aliens. And by failing to act on legislation or, even better, a clarifying constitutional amendment aimed at correcting the interpretation of citizenship by birth, Congress in effect rewards law breakers and punishes those who have chosen to follow the rules and immigrate legally.

Solutions

The Constitution, in Article One, Section 8, gives Congress the power to "establish an uniform Rule of Naturalization."

Bills introduced but never passed

Fears that U.S.-born children of illegal immigrants could serve as links to permit legal residency and eventual citizenship for family members who would otherwise be ineligible to remain in the country have led to bills being introduced from time to time that challenged the now default interpretation of the citizenship clause. Most have sought to actively and explicitly deny citizenship at birth to U.S.-born children of foreign visitors or illegal aliens. None as yet have been passed.

One example among many, the "Birthright Citizenship Act of 2009" introduced in the House of Representatives by Representative Nathan Deal of Georgia, was an attempt to exclude U.S.-born children of illegal immigrants from being considered subject to the jurisdiction of the United States for purposes of the citizenship clause. A similar proposal named the "Birthright Citizenship Act of 2011" was introduced in the House in January 2011 by Representative Steve King of Iowa and in the Senate in April 2011 by Senator David Vita (R–Louisiana).

Since an act of Congress challenging the accepted interpretation of the citizenship clause might be ruled unconstitutional by courts choosing to rely on *Wong Kim Ark* as a precedent, proposals have also been made to amend the Constitution to clarify the Fourteenth Amendment's language and deny citizenship to U.S.-born children of illegal aliens or foreign visitors. For example, Senator Vita introduced a Senate Joint Resolution for such an amendment in 2010 and 2011. It was nixed in the 2015 deal with Senate Democrats to curb human trafficking.

Rep. Steve King (R–Arizona) reintroduced such legislation in 2015. But even if such a bill were successful, it is all too likely that a future Court would construe it as invalid by misreading the Fourteenth Amendment to formally establish the citizenship of one born here of a mother who was in the U.S. illegally or of parents both of whom were citizens of another country at the time of birth.

Seventh Circuit Judge Richard Posner, reacting to *Oforji v. Ashcroft,* stated, "Congress would not be flouting the Constitution if it amended the Immigration and Nationality Act to put an end to the nonsense." Congress routinely authors legislation aimed at clarifying the scope of the Second Amendment, so why could it not do the same for the Fourteenth?

Andy Semotiuk, writing in *Forbes* in 2016, proposes some solutions:

W1-AO
http://www.forbes.com/sites/andyjsemotiuk/2016/10/05/the-citizenship-and-immigration-problems-of-anchor-babies-and-surrogacy/

In 2015, Senator David Vitter introduced legislation to make the necessary clarifications of what "subject to the jurisdiction thereof" really means.

W1-AP
http://www.usatoday.com/story/opinion/2015/08/20/birthright-citizenship-Fourteenth-amendment-sen-david-vitter-editorials-debates/32082627

President Donald Trump called for an end to birthright citizenship during his 2016 campaign. A president could issue an executive order to end the current misapplication of the Fourteenth Amendment. John Feere at the Center for Immigration Studies concludes that executive action could put this problem to bed:

W1-AQ http://cis.org/opedsandArticles/feere-how-trump-could-change-birthright-citizenship

A petition to send to your representative and senators can be found at

W1-AR https://www.petition2congress.com/ctas/stop-automatic-citizenship-through-anchor-babies

An amendment perhaps

Because of *Wong* and the misapplication by the U.S. government of the comments by Justice Brennan in his footnote to *Plyler v. Doe*, it may take a constitutional amendment to end drop-in citizenship. I propose:

> *With respect to the Fourteenth Amendment of this Constitution, the phrase "subject to the jurisdiction thereof" shall be construed to exclude from citizenship persons born in the United States or its territories of parents neither of which is at the time of birth is either a legal resident or a citizen of the United States.*

Following its adoption, appropriate legislation at the federal and state levels can be enacted to prevent further damage and return a common-sense meaning to the term "citizen of the United States."

For further reading and action

¡Adios, America! by Ann Coulter; 2015, Regnery Publishing

W1-AS https://www.goodreads.com/book/show/25437276-

adios-america

The Center for Immigration Studies, Washington, D.C., lobbies for sensible immigration policies and does extensive research on immigration issues.

W1-AT https://www.cis.org

The Federation for Immigration Reform (FAIR), Washington, D.C., is a leading activist organization for sensible immigration policies.

W1-AU https://www.fairus.org

2~*Steward Machine Company v. Davis* and *Helvering v. Davis* (1937)

[Aid to the States was] "encumbering the national government beyond its wisdom to comprehend, or its ability to administer." — Calvin Coolidge

What, when it comes to government, do we mean by the term "general welfare?" To an originalist reader of the Constitution, it refers to activities and expenditures by the federal government that benefit society as a whole, such as defense, diplomacy, a postal system, highways and ports, and a judicial system. It is unlikely that its drafters meant payments to other governmental entities and individuals other than for labor or goods and services for which there was a contract for provision to the federal government in the course of its operations.

In addition to the preamble, the term "general welfare" is found in the tax and spending clause (Article I, Section 8, Clause 1):

> [The Congress shall have Power] To lay and collect Taxes, Duties, Imposts and Excises, to pay the Debts and provide for the common Defense and general Welfare of the United States; but all Duties, Imposts and Excises shall be uniform throughout the United States.

At the outset, there were differences of opinion about just

what "general welfare" meant to the scope of federal spending. Madison held that the enumeration of expenditures that followed in this section indicated that spending should be restricted to these categories. Hamilton held that the term "general welfare" could allow almost any expenditure that would benefit the country. Madison ridiculed Hamilton's view by pointing out that the Convention had put much work into creating a list of enumerated powers so it was unlikely that "general welfare" was a catchall to allow spending on just about anything.

Madison's view pretty much prevailed until the New Deal, when payments to individuals other than employees or for the provision of contracted goods and services became part of a new entitlement mentality.

Compromising commentary led the way

To understand both decisions in this chapter, it is necessary to visit a decision a year earlier, *United States v. Butler*. At issue was whether certain provisions of the Agricultural Adjustment Act of 1933 conflicted with the Constitution. The Act imposed a tax on processors of farm products, with the proceeds to be paid to farmers who would reduce their operational area and crop production. The intent of the act was to decrease production and thus increase the prices of certain farm products.

The Court held that the so-called tax was not valid because the payments to farmers were coupled with unlawful and oppressively coercive contracts and the proceeds were earmarked for the benefit of farmers complying with the prescribed conditions. The Court also held that making the payment of a government subsidy to a farmer conditional on the reduction of planned crops went beyond the powers of the federal government. So far, so good. But the commentary led to a more expansive view of what qualifies for federal spending:

> The [general welfare] clause confers a power separate and distinct from those later enumerated[,] is not restricted in meaning by the grant of them, and Congress consequently has a substantive power to tax and to appropriate, limited only by the requirement that it shall be exercised to provide for the general welfare of the United States. … It results that the power of Congress to authorize expenditure of public moneys for public purposes is not limited by the direct grants of legislative power found in the Constitution.

The die was cast. The first instance of implementing a payment scheme for individuals was in unemployment insurance cases. Since there was a connection between such payments and previous work, the view that such payouts were not an unearned handout was plausible. But the payouts could become a claim on the public purse if claims come to exceed the total of employee vesting. The Social Security Act of 1935 ushered in the entitlement state in the form of unemployment insurance and payouts not directly related to earnings. The two cases discussed below sealed the new spending scheme. ("Davis" in these cases are not the same person.)

Steward Machine v. Davis (1937)

Coercing the states and expanding "general welfare"

Steward Machine is an Alabama manufacturer of supplies for the coal and iron ore mining industry and later iron rolling, steel, movable bridge machinery, lock and dam, and heavy industrial equipment. The business is still family-owned.

In 1936 it sued the IRS (where the collector of revenue was Harwell Davis) on the grounds that the Social Security Act went beyond the powers granted to the federal government in the Constitution and involved coercion of the states in contravention of the Tenth Amendment in that it called for a surrender by the states of powers essential to their quasi-sovereign existence.

Steward Machine did not prevail in the lower courts and appealed. In 1937 the Supreme Court upheld the unemployment compensation provisions of the Act, which had established a national taxing structure designed to induce states to adopt laws for funding and payment of unemployment compensation.

The Court further ruled that federal funds raised for possible unemployment payouts were neither a trust fund nor insurance, but rather an excise tax, even though heretofore excise taxes could be assessed only on objects of consumption. (The appealed decision of the lower court held that this tax was an excise tax and therefore constitutional.)

Unemployment compensation in the Social Security Act

The unemployment compensation provisions of the Social Security Act of 1935 established a tax on employers. If, however, a state had established an approved unemployment compensation plan, the taxpayer was allowed to credit up to 90% of the federal tax paid to the state unemployment fund. The effect of the Act was to establish a taxing structure that induced states to adopt consistent laws for funding and payment of unemployment compensation.

The central issues in *Steward* were whether the tax coerced the states and whether Congress had the power to enact it. The critical holding regarding the excise tax in the Social Security Act was that the excise did not constitute coercion of the states in contravention of the Tenth Amendment or violate restrictions implicit in a federal form of government. Key was the reasoning that even if excise taxes were a form of pressure on the states, the Act was still valid, and the credit and tax in combination were not coercive to a degree that would destroy or diminish the autonomy of the states.

Referring to current conditions rather than the Constitution

The majority ruling noted that the states were unable to give what the justices saw as needed relief from high unemployment and the threat of starvation and implicitly incorporated the commentary in *Butler* that Congress has a "separate and distinct" power to tax and spend that is "not limited by the direct grants of legislative power found in the Constitution."

The Court found for the government, 5–4. The majority opinion was written by Justice Benjamin Cardozo. Cardozo, of Portuguese descent, had been appointed by President Herbert Hoover in 1932 to succeed Oliver Wendell Holmes Jr. Cardozo served on the Court until 1938 and formed part of the liberal bloc of justices known as the Three Musketeers. He wrote the Court's majority opinion in both these cases and in other notable cases such as *Nixon v. Condon*. One of Cardozo's tutors as a child was Horatio Alger. Cardozo went into law partly to elevate the family name after his father, a judge on the Supreme Court of New York, was implicated in a judicial corruption scandal. Cardozo attended Columbia Law School for two years but left without graduating.

In his opinion, Cardozo contended that concern about coercion was not valid as it was impossible to distinguish between compulsion and inducement if the object of a federal law was a national end (general welfare) and related to the tax itself. The decision also punted on the question of whether Social Security was an excise tax. It declared, "We find it unnecessary to make a choice between the arguments, and so leave the question open."

The dissents

The four dissenters had a much better grasp of federalism. The essence of the dissents was that the Social Security Act of 1935 went beyond the powers granted to the federal government in the Constitution. Imposing a tax that could be avoided only by contributing to a state unemployment compensation fund was effectively coercing each state to make law creating such a fund. Among the points made by the dissenters were the following:

> The Act unduly interferes with the orderly government of the state by her own people and otherwise offends the federal Constitution.

> There is no authority in the Constitution for making the federal government the "great almoner" of public charity throughout the United States.

> Article 1, Section 8 is not a substantive general power to provide for the welfare of the United States but rather a limitation on the grant of power of Congress to raise money by taxes, duties, imposts, and excises.

> The Constitution grants to the United States no power to pay unemployed persons or to require the states to enact laws or to raise or disburse money for that purpose.

> The implicit threat in this encroachment upon the administrative functions of the states is that greater encroachments will follow.

These comments reflect the Madisonian view. Unfortunately, in this case, he, and we, lost.

Helvering v. Davis (1937)

Later that year, the ruling in *Helvering v. Davis* further enabled New Deal programs, creating broad new powers for the federal government, by misreading the general welfare clause to permit expenditures other than for the enumerated operational activities of the central government. Thus, the stage was set for welfare to individuals and politically purposed federal spending for local and special interests.

The Case

This case arose when a minor shareholder of the Edison Electric Illuminating Company of Boston, George Davis, brought a derivative action to restrain the company from making payments and deductions required by the 1935 Social Security Act on the grounds that by complying Edison was improperly robbing him of part of his equity and the law was unconstitutional as a tax not allowed to the federal government. He sought an injunction in the First District Court and a declaration that the Act was void. The court permitted the Commissioner of the Internal Revenue Service, Guy Helvering, to represent Edison Electric. The court ruled against Davis, who appealed to the Court of Appeals for the First Circuit. That court held in Davis's favor, so Helvering appealed to the Supreme Court in a case. The case was retitled *Helvering v. Davis*.

In this ruling, Social Security was deemed constitutionally permissible as an exercise of the federal power to spend for the general welfare and not in contravention of the Tenth Amendment's limiting of the federal government to enumerated powers. The Court defended the constitutionality of the Social Security Act, requiring only that welfare spending should be for a common benefit as distinguished from some mere local purpose. It also affirmed a district court decree that held that the tax upon employees was not at issue and that the tax upon employers was constitutional.

The majority opinion, written by Justice Cardozo, supported the right of Congress to interpret the "general welfare" clause. Some excerpts:

> Congress may spend money in aid of the "general welfare" ... There have been great statesmen in

> our history who have stood for other views... The line must still be drawn between one welfare and another, between particular and general. Where this shall be placed cannot be known through a formula in advance of the event... The discretion belongs to Congress, unless the choice is clearly wrong, a display of arbitrary power, not an exercise of judgment. This is now familiar law.

The decision went on to cite the results of research of various government agencies and congressional committees. It continued:

> The problem is plainly national in area and dimensions. Moreover, laws of the separate states cannot deal with it effectively. Congress, at least, had a basis for that belief. States and local governments are often lacking in the resources that are necessary to finance an adequate program of security for the aged.

More studies were then cited regarding the limitations of state resources for the needy and dependent.

Side note of interest

Joining the decision was Justice Harlan Stone, who, during the drafting of the legislation had advised Secretary Frances Perkins that the constitutionality of Social Security could be based on "the taxing power of the Federal Government, my dear; the taxing power is sufficient for everything you want and need."

Findings

So, the Court ruled that Social Security was not a contributory insurance program, saying, "The proceeds of both the employee and employer taxes are to be paid into the Treasury like any other internal revenue generally, and are not earmarked in any way."

With its detailed references to various studies, this decision amounts to an exercise in promoting a public policy with which the majority agreed rather than in seeking guidance from the clear text of the Constitution.

Consequences

The Tenth Amendment embodies federalism—the idea that federal and state governments have separate areas of activity and that federal responsibilities are "few and defined," as James Madison noted. Historically, federalism acted as a safeguard of American freedoms.

But *Steward* and *Helvering* marked the beginning of the idea that Congress could use the spending clause, under the umbrella of "general welfare," to regulate state laws through incentives and encouragement—but not coercion. Before *Steward*, Congress could regulate only commercial economic activity; after these cases, Congress could control the actions of state governments. It has since been common for Congress to tie grants-in-aid with requirements and restrictions upon the states.

There were fifteen grants-in-aid programs in 1930 and 1,200 by 2018. Lyndon Johnson's "Great Society" saw an explosion of federal aid for housing, urban renewal, education, health care, and many other areas. The phenomenon is bipartisan. Nixon said he wanted to reverse the flow of power and resources from Washington to the states and communities, but little progress was made. Reagan made some progress but was restrained by a Democrat-controlled House, and what progress he made was reversed after he left office. The Bushes did not seem to be interested in reducing spending. Obamacare added a range of new aid programs, and it also involved a massive expansion of Medicaid, already the most expensive federal aid program.

This 2018 study from the Mercatus Center at George Mason University has two charts that show the expansion of various types of aid programs since 1960:

W2-AA https://www.mercatus.org/system/files/Federal-grant-aid-state-and-local-chart-analysis-pdf.pdf

By 2017, aid programs numbered over 1,200, and spending on aid to the states was projected to exceed $641 billion, making aid the third largest item in the federal budget after Social Security and national defense. The deficit in Trump's third fiscal year is over one trillion dollars!

Disadvantages of this aid regime

Federal aid stifles policy diversity and innovation in the states, which can be laboratories of democracy to test different ways to govern. Federal grants reduce state diversity and innovation because they come with one-size-fits-all mandates. Some examples of bad results:

> The 55-mile-per-hour national speed limit that ignored road travel differences among the states.

> The No-Child-Left-Behind education law of 2002 that accomplished nothing but a substantial loss of local power.

> The Davis–Bacon labor rules that increased construction costs on government investments, such as highway projects, by mandating prevailing union wages.

> Matching requirements have induced excessive state spending and continuous program expansion. Such fiscal irresponsibility is one of the many negative consequences of the Race to the Top program and the Common Core Standards Initiative.

> If states opt out of new aid programs for sound policy reasons, their residents would still have to pay federal taxes to support federal aid spending in other states.

> Many grant programs are ineffective and wasteful. Do we need spending at the national level for such things as nursing workforce diversity, boating safety financial assistance, or healthy marriages?

> There is no relationship between federal taxes received from taxpayers in a state and the aid the state gets back. Political struggles can tweak the allocations.

> Overhead for federal handling and supervision is a cost that reduces the value of money sent to Washington and then returned, in part.

> A massive federal aid system takes time that federal officials could spend on truly national issues because they must focus on state and local issues.

> Federal aid has made it difficult for citizens to figure out which level of government is responsible for particular policy outcomes.

> Federal aid confuses the distinction between issues of national scope, which may justify federal action, and problems that are merely common to the states, which will not justify federal action because individual states, acting individually or together, can effectively deal with them.

"General welfare" would be better interpreted as a restriction on federal spending to require that expenditures benefit the country as a whole and not specific entities. A federal check to you or any entity other than for services performed or goods purchased is not a national public expenditure.

Solutions

Even though many know the federal aid complex has many failings, a web of special interest groups blocks reforms. Those groups include the hundreds of trade associations that represent the recipients of federal aid and the millions of state and local employees that depend on federal aid to pay their salaries.

The aid system thrives because it maximizes benefits to politicians, not because it creates good governance. The system allows politicians at each level of government to take credit for spending while blaming other levels of government for program failures and high tax burdens. The federal aid system has been called a "triumph of expenditure without responsibility."

The aid system should be gradually phased out altogether and possibly combined with a meaningful decrease in the federal income tax. With the national debt in the double-digit trillions and the current (2020) annual deficit higher than the gross national product, there is every reason to start cutting federal spending on state and local activities. "Federal money" is, of course, money that taxpayers send to Washington (or that is borrowed), some of which they can't recover unless their state jumps through the federal hoop. Is this any way to run a federal republic in a free society?

As with most Supreme Court cases, there are no remedies outside of an amendment or another challenge that would overturn this and related decisions and restore the Madisonian view that "general welfare" did not allow any expenditure outside the enumerated powers of the federal government. Also helpful would be Americans reviving their traditional respect for liberty and freedom from big government in most aspects of their lives.

For further reading

A letter by Thomas Jefferson on misuse of the general welfare clause:

W2-AB https://tenthamendmentcenter.com/2014/12/28/thomas-jefferson-on-the-misuse-of-the-commerce-and-general-welfare-clauses/

Federalist Paper #45, probably by Madison, which defends the need for more powers for the federal government, but not to the extent that states do not retain significant powers:

W2-AC https://www.thefederalistpapers.org/founders/madison/james-madison-federalist-papers-45

The Tenth Amendment Center has an article explaining the original purpose, via Madison, of the general welfare clause and the limits of federal authority in the Constitution:

W2-AD
https://tenthamendmentcenter.com/2017/06/05/general-welfare-and-common-defense-explained-by-james-madison/

A 1998 article on Social Security by Michael Tanner of the Cato Institute:

W2-AE https://www.cato.org/publications/commentary/is-there-right-social-security

A history of differing views of the general welfare clause is this 2011 Heritage Foundation article by John C. Eastman:

W2-AF https://www.heritage.org/the-constitution/report/enough-enough-why-general-welfare-limits-spending

A 2013 article from Downsizing Government on federal grants-in-aid presents a full history of this type of federal spending and eight good ways to make deep cuts:

W2-AG
https://www.downsizinggovernment.org/fiscal-federalism

Saving Congress from Itself by James L. Buckley; 2014, Encounter Books

W2-AH
https://reason.com/2015/01/13/judge-james-l-buckley-saving-c

3~*West Coast Hotel v. Parrish* (1937)

Economic freedom cannot be sacrificed if political freedom is to be preserved. — Herbert Hoover

Economic rights are those powers of action and decision that a person or nonpublic entity uses to further their interests and well-being that, when exercised, do not infringe on the person or property of another person or nonpublic entity. Until the New Deal era, such rights were usually respected by the courts, particularly after the 1905 case *Lochner v. New York*, in which the Court ruled that a bakery could not be forced by state law to limit the hours its employees worked.

The *Lochner* era: the freedom to contract

Liberty to contract is an economic right; an example is an employer and employee coming to a mutual agreement on the terms of employment. Over the thirty-two years of the "Lochner era," the Court struck down numerous worker- and consumer-protection laws. A majority of the Court usually held that the Fourteenth Amendment guaranteed a "freedom of contract" that overrides laws designed to protect workers or consumers. An example is the 1923 case *Adkins v. Children's Hospital*, in which the Court voided a federal minimum-wage law for women as an unconstitutional infringement of the liberty of contract, as protected by the due process clause of the Fifth and Fourteenth Amendments. (The Fifth Amendment reads, "No person shall be deprived of life, liberty, or property, without due process of law." The Fourteenth Amendment reads, "No State shall deprive any person of life, liberty, or property, without due process of law.")

This view continued to inform Supreme Court decisions through the Great Depression and to the beginning of the New Deal, which invalidated numerous worker and consumer protection laws. And just months before *West Coast Hotel v. Parrish*, the Court struck down a similar minimum-wage law from New York in *Morehead v. New York ex rel. Tipaldo*.

In response to the invalidation of much of the legislation that Roosevelt favored, he proposed changing the number of Supreme Court justices, which his opponents characterized as the "court-packing plan." It was evident that this bill was intended to dilute the influence of the older justices, who saw much of the New Deal as unconstitutional.

Freedom to contract curtailed

Late in the summer of 1933, Elsie Lee, a woman of forty who would soon become Elsie Parrish, took a job as a chambermaid at the Cascadian Hotel in Wenatchee, a market center for a beautiful recreation area reaching from the Columbia Valley to the Cascades and the country's foremost apple-growing region. Here, in the land of Winesaps and Jonathans, Elsie worked irregularly over the next year and a half cleaning toilets and sweeping rugs for an hourly wage of twenty-two cents, later raised to a quarter.

When she was discharged in May 1935, she asked for back pay—the difference between what she had received and what she would have gotten if she had been paid each week at the state minimum wage required for her occupation. The Cascadian, which was owned by the West Coast Hotel Company, offered to settle for a total of $17.00, but she rejected the offer. Instead, she, together with her new husband, Ernest, brought suit for all that she was due according to the provisions of a statute that had been enacted by Washington state a quarter of a century before when the state legislature took steps to wipe out sweatshops. The 1913 act declared it "unlawful to employ women or minors … under conditions of labor detrimental to their health or morals; and … to employ women workers in any industry … at wages which are not adequate for their maintenance." The law established a commission that was authorized to convene employers, employees, and representatives of the public, who would recommend a wage standard that conformed with the provisions of the act.

Upon receiving that recommendation, the commission was to issue an order stipulating the minimum wage that must be paid. The statute had been challenged in the courts twice, and on both occasions the Washington Supreme Court had upheld it. So, Elsie Parrish appeared to have an airtight case. But the trial court, citing *Adkins* as precedent, ruled for the hotel. The Washington Supreme Court reversed, finding in favor of Parrish, so the hotel appealed to the U.S. Supreme Court.

The decision

Departing from the prevailing understanding of the freedom to contract, the Court in *West Coast Hotel v. Parrish* upheld the constitutionality of the state of Washington's minimum-wage legislation. The Court ruled that the Constitution permits the restriction of liberty to contract by state law where such restriction protects the community, health, and safety of vulnerable groups. The decision took issue with the idea that the Constitution provides for freedom to contract. Instead, the majority decision stated that the Constitution

speaks of liberty and prohibits the deprivation of liberty without due process of law. In prohibiting that deprivation, the Constitution does not recognize an absolute and uncontrollable liberty. Liberty in each of its phases has its history and connotation. But the liberty safeguarded is liberty in a social organization which requires the protection of law against the evils which menace the health, safety, morals, and welfare of the people. Liberty under the Constitution is thus necessarily subject to the restraints of due process, and regulation which is reasonable in relation to its subject and is adopted in the interests of the community is due process.

The dissents

The four dissenters made these points:

> The meaning of the Constitution does not change with the ebb and flow of economic events and, therefore, the only way to change the intended purpose would be through an amendment.

> Freedom of contract should be the rule and restraint upon that freedom the exception, and case law illustrated that the power to abridge that freedom to contract could be justified only by extraordinary circumstances.

> There is no state interest in fixing wages for women and doing so is essentially gender discrimination, as both sexes have the same capability to contract out their labor.

A significant change in jurisprudence

The decision was a surprise to all because one justice, Owen Roberts, who previously had sided with the conservatives in pro-*Lochner* decisions, changed his stance in this case and voted to uphold the minimum-wage law. Just a few months before, he had voted to strike down a similar minimum-wage law in the *Morehead* case. The reasons for Roberts's change of mind remains unclear (especially as Roberts burned all his papers on retirement), but one consequencc was the derailing of Roosevelt's court "reform" bill. Roberts's move was referred to at the time as "the switch in time that saved nine."

Consequences

The Court was making policy in *West Coast v.Parrish* rather than defending liberties expressed and implied in the Constitution. The decision marked the end of the Lochner era and increased jurisprudential deference to current political preferences.

Relevant subsequent cases include *United States v. Carolene Products* (1938), in which economic regulations were deemed not to violate the due process clause if they pass the "rational basis test." (See next chapter.)

Another is *United States v. Darby* (1941), in which the Court upheld the Fair Labor Standards Act of 1938, which mandated minimum wages under the commerce clause. This case significantly increased Congress's latitude to enact economic regulations. The National Constitution Center summarizes the case:

W3-AA https://constitutioncenter.org/timeline/html/cw09_12200.html

Parrish enhanced the power of government at all levels to inflict the distortions and adverse consequences of minimum-wage laws. This observation is one of many points made by Richard Epstein in a 1988 article in the University of Chicago Law School's *Journal:*:

W3-AB http://chicagounbound.uchicago.edu/cgi/viewcontent.cgi?article=2284&context=journal_articles

David Bernstein, in the Volokh Conspiracy blog, wrote about how *Parrish* was a significant factor in leveraging "living constitution" jurisprudence over originalism:

W3-AC http://volokh.com/2012/10/10/the-significance-of-west-coast-hotel-v-parrish-originalism-vs-living-constitutionalism/

Of course, the "living constitution" approach to jurisprudence means there is no fixed reference point for the basic law of the land, and it is a surrender of the people to the policy preferences of five unelected lawyers in a black robe.

Solutions

With there being many state laws regarding employment in the private sector, there is no easy path to restoring Lochner-style liberty to the employee–employer relationship. But Congress could amend the 1938 Fair Labor Standards Act (FLSA) to eliminate the federal minimum-wage section as an example.

Hardly any employees do not make more than the current $7.25 federal minimum wage. The five states that do not have a minimum-wage law could assess whether or not to enact one. As well argued by Mark Hendrickson in an article listed below, minimum-wage laws, federal or state, are counterproductive.

For further reading

The Constitution Besieged: The Rise and Demise of Lochner Era Police Powers Jurisprudence by Howard Gillman; 1993, Duke University Press:

W3-AD https://read.dukeupress.edu/books/book/1922/The-Constitution-BesiegedThe-Rise-amp-Demise-of

Rehabilitating Lochner by David Bernstein; 2011, University of Chicago Press:

W3-AE https://www.independent.org/publications/tir/article.asp?id=871

Article "The Folly of Minimum Wage Laws" by Mark Hendrickson in the *Mises Wire* blog:

W3-AF https://mises.org/wire/folly-minimum-wage-laws

4~*United States v. Carolene Products Company* (1938)

The only way a government can be of service to national prosperity is by keeping its hands off.
—Ayn Rand

This case is best known for a footnote in which the Court explained its "rational basis" (lesser level of) scrutiny of economic regulations. The decision and its *obiter dicta* had the effect of diminishing the protection of rights that were not enumerated. The case continued the trend inaugurated the year before of affording less than strict scrutiny of laws affecting economic rights. It also laid out three areas where courts were to apply strict scrutiny going forward. So, some rights are more equal than others, as Orwell might have put it.

The strict scrutiny standard of judicial review applies to laws that either interfere with the exercise of a fundamental constitutional right or discriminate based on a suspect classification (e.g., race). A law reviewed under this standard is presumed to be unconstitutional and will not be upheld unless its proponents can demonstrate that it is necessary to promote a compelling state (governmental) interest. Few, if any, laws reviewed under this standard survive. At the opposite end is the rational basis standard of review, which applies to almost all other legislation. Under this standard, a law is presumed to be constitutional and will be upheld so long as it has a rational relationship to any legitimate state (governmental) purpose. Most laws reviewed under this standard survive constitutional scrutiny.

Congress bends to industry pressure; Court says OK

Under pressure from the evaporated and condensed milk lobbies, Congress in 1923 passed the federal Filled Milk Act, which prohibited interstate commerce in canned milk in which coconut or other vegetable oils were substituted for natural butterfat in milk to reduce cost and lengthen shelf life. (Refrigerators were not so common back then.) There is little to suggest that is purchasers did not know what they were buying. Illinois, the home of Carolene Products, had no law against this product, so the company continued to make Milnut.

The Carolene Products Company was indicted under this law in 1935. The lower court found Carolene to be "an adulterated article of food, injurious to the public health" under the statute. The defendant company appealed, challenging the constitutionality of the law on both commerce clause and due process grounds. The United States District Court for the Southern District of Illinois granted the defendant's motion, and the Seventh Circuit Court of Appeals affirmed the District Court's ruling.

Before the *Parrish* decision in the previous year, the Court had routinely found statutes that limited "freedom to contract" or regulated economic activity unconstitutional based on the due process clauses of the Fifth and Fourteenth Amendments.

In *United States v. Carolene Products Company*, the Supreme Court upheld the constitutionality of the regulatory scheme. It deferred to the expertise and findings of the legislature even though the defendant had had no opportunity to challenge the legislative findings in a judicial proceeding. In so ruling, the

Court had to abandon the presumption of unconstitutionality that it had applied in earlier cases like *Lochner v. New York* (1905).

In *Lochner,* the Court had established a principle of safeguarding private business from government encroachment and the right to contract between employer and employee. The issue was about laws restricting hours per week that an employer, the baker Lochner, could require of his employees. *Carolene Products* implicitly overruled *Lochner* and was the death knell for the doctrine of substantive due process as applied to economic regulation.

Perhaps this turn could have been seen to be coming. In a 1934 case, *Nebbia v. New York*, the Court upheld a New York milk price stabilization law. And in the previous term, the Court had dramatically enlarged the scope of activities considered to be in, or to affect, interstate commerce. It had also altered its settled jurisprudence in the area of substantive due process, the doctrine dealing with rights not enumerated in the Constitution.

These changes meant that many New Deal programs that the Court would previously have struck down as unconstitutional would henceforth be found constitutional.

In *Carolene Products,* the majority held that the law was "presumptively constitutional" and properly within legislative discretion and hence was not for the courts to overrule because it was supported by substantial public-health evidence and was not arbitrary or irrational. That is, the Court applied the "rational basis" test.

Footnote Four

The second paragraph of footnote four stated the rationale for the decision:

> It is unnecessary to consider now whether legislation which restricts those political processes which can ordinarily be expected to bring about repeal of undesirable legislation, is to be subjected to more exacting judicial scrutiny under the general prohibitions of the Fourteenth Amendment than are most other types of legislation.

Since the Court was bailing out of defending the right to practice a trade or enter into contracts, it must have felt it necessary to give assurances that it was not abandoning strict review in certain noneconomic cases. So, the footnote outlined three categories of cases it would consider under a more stringent scrutiny regime. None were economic, but many subsequent civil rights cases were based on this paragraph.

Aftermath

Carolene Products president Charles Hauser was subsequently convicted (in 1943) and spent time in prison before being pardoned by Roosevelt in 1945. In 1972 the Filled Milk Act was struck down by the same district court that initially ruled that it passed the rational basis test. Milnut was relabeled as Milnot in 1939 and later acquired by the J.M. Smucker Company, which sold it to Eagle Family Foods in 2015. The saga is a case of a law that should not have been passed and a subsequent court decision that should have come down on the opposite side.

Consequences

The Ninth Amendment states that "[t]he enumeration in the Constitution of certain rights shall not be construed to deny or disparage others retained by the People." The right to earn an honest living would surely be one. But federal courts grew to give short shrift to cases where a business owner felt his rights in offering a valid product or service were curtailed or prohibited.

Lee Optical framed

An example is a 1955 case, *Williamson v. Lee Optical*, in which the Court held that state laws regulating business would be subject only to rational basis review and that the Court need not contemplate all possible reasons for legislation.

The optician plaintiff brought suit to have a 1953 Oklahoma law declared unconstitutional and to enjoin state officials from enforcing it. The law contained provisions making it unlawful for any person not a licensed optometrist or ophthalmologist to fit lenses to a frame or to duplicate or replace into frames lenses or other optical appliances except upon written prescriptive authority of an Oklahoma licensed ophthalmologist or optometrist. This law required every individual seeking to have eyeglasses made, repaired, or refitted to obtain a prescription. The law exempted sellers of ready-to-wear eyeglasses but impacted unlicensed opticians. It was thus challenged on due process grounds for arbitrary interference with an optician's right to do business as well as on equal protection grounds.

The district court ruled that portions of the act violated the due process clause of the Fourteenth Amendment and that other parts violated the equal protection clause of the Fourteenth Amendment. The state appealed.

Using rational basis review, the Supreme Court found that the Oklahoma state legislature had a legitimate interest in requiring a prescription from a licensed optometrist or ophthalmologist for all fittings. Although opticians were qualified to refit lenses without prescriptions, the Court reasoned that requiring prescriptions in every case would encourage more frequent eye examinations, which might enable early detection of more serious eye conditions. Consequently, where a legitimate governmental interest lies, as reasoned by the Court, the law can survive a due process challenge. Clearly, this decision was based on the public policy preferences of the Court's majority, not constitutional rights.

Justice William O. Douglas wrote the majority opinion. Douglas had been a law-and-order conservative in the 1940s when he still hoped to become president, but he became more sensitive to the rights of religious minorities to court the Catholic vote. By the 1950s, he had turned himself into a staunch civil libertarian, but his opinions became increasingly self-indulgent. "I'm ready to bend the law in favor of the environment and against the corporations," he boasted. His most famous opinion, *Griswold v. Connecticut*, located a right to privacy in "penumbras, formed by emanations" from the Bill of Rights. In evolving from a pro-government advocate in the 1940s to an icon of liberalism in the 1960s, Douglas became a champion of the rights of privacy and free speech and of the environment. While doing so, "Wild Bill" lived up to his nickname by racking up more marriages, more divorces, and more attempts to impeach him than any other member of the Court. In his last year on the Court, he suffered from delusions stemming from a stroke but refused to step down, so the other justices stopped counting his votes in sessions to decide which cases to hear. The full story on Douglas, good and bad, can be found in "*Wild Bill: The Life and Times of William O. Douglas* by Bruce Allen Murphy (Random House, 2003).

Writing for the Court in *Lee Optical*, Douglas spelled out the standard for determining whether a law survives a due process challenge, stating that "the law need not be in every respect logically consistent with its aims to be constitutional. It is enough that there is an evil at hand for correction, and that it might be thought that the particular legislative measure was a rational way to correct it." He further wrote: "The day is gone when this court uses the due process clause of the Fourteenth Amendment to strike down state laws, regulatory of business and industrial conditions, because they may be unwise, improvident, or out of harmony with a particular school of thought."

The Court summarily addressed the equal protection issue, explaining: "The prohibition of the equal protection clause goes no further than invidious discrimination. We cannot say that this point has been reached here."

Special interests

One result of this avoidance of considering unenumerated rights has been a plethora of special interest legislation. Few occupations are too innocent in the eyes of legislators to escape regulation. Examples of challenges to such legislation that failed to win in the courts are Louisiana laws requiring a license to do flower arranging, an

Oklahoma law requiring sales of caskets to be made only by licensed funeral directors, and an Iowa law requiring a license to practice or teach African-style hair braiding.

Solutions

There is no remedy for unreasonable restrictions on economic liberty other than the victims of excessive regulation being ready to sue. The Institute for Justice does a terrific job of defending economic rights.

W4-AA https://www.ij.org/pillar/economic-liberty

For further reading

Article: "The True Story of *Carolene Products*" by Geoffrey P. Miller, in *Supreme Court Review*, 1987; University of Chicago Press. Possible access fee.

W4-AB https://www.journals.uchicago.edu/doi/abs/10.1086/scr.1987.3109594

Article: "The Footnote" by Jack M. Balkin; Yale (1988)

W4-AC http://digitalcommons.law.yale.edu/fss_papers/287/

Restoring the Lost Constitution: The Presumption of Liberty by Randy E. Barnett; 2005, Princeton University Press

W4-AD http://press.princeton.edu/titles/10118.html

Josh Blackman blog: pictures and ephemera about Carolene Products Company

W4-AE http://joshblackman.com/blog/?s=CAROLENE

5~*Wickard v. Filburn* (1942)

The powers delegated by the proposed Constitution to the federal government are few and defined. Those which are to remain in the State governments are numerous and indefinite. —James Madison

A key failing of the Articles of Confederation was the propensity of the states to erect protectionist trade barriers. When the Framers met in Philadelphia in 1787 and wrote the Constitution that governs us today, they addressed that failure and through the commerce and privileges and immunities clauses created a national free-trade zone. Thus, the *original* purpose of the commerce clause was primarily to eliminate trade barriers among the states. The damage that ensued from *Wickard v. Filburn* is more significant than its public awareness would suggest. This 1942 case is important in that it stretched the federal government's power over the individual to new levels.

The federal arm reaches to the last acre

Roscoe Curtiss Filburn was a farmer near Dayton, Ohio. His farm was a part of his grandparents' farmstead, which originally totaled 640 acres. On his remaining ninety-five acres, Filburn grew wheat, raised poultry and dairy cows, and sold milk and eggs. Some of the wheat he grew for family use and to feed farm animals.

But the U.S. Department of Agriculture fined him for growing more wheat than he was allowed to grow under the Agricultural Adjustment Act of 1938, which was passed under the power of Congress to regulate interstate commerce.

Filburn pointed out that his wheat wasn't sold, so it didn't enter any commerce, interstate or otherwise. Therefore, the federal government had no right to tell him how much wheat (which never left his farm) he could grow.

The Ninth Amendment to the Constitution says, "The enumeration in the Constitution, of certain rights, shall not be construed to deny or disparage others retained by the people." So, you might think that Filburn made a valid point.

But a majority of justices on the Supreme Court thought otherwise. Even though the wheat on Filburn's farm never entered the market, the fact that "it supplies a need of the man who grew it which would otherwise be reflected by purchases in the open market meant that it affected interstate commerce. So did the fact that the home-grown wheat could potentially enter the market."

The implications of this kind of reasoning reached far beyond farmers and wheat. Once it was established that the federal government could regulate not only interstate commerce itself but anything with any potential effect on interstate commerce, the Ninth Amendment's limitations on the powers of the federal government virtually disappeared.

Over the years, "interstate commerce" became magic words to justify almost any expansion of the federal government's power, in defiance of the Ninth and Tenth Amendments. That concept was what the Obama administration depended on to get the Supreme Court to uphold the administration's power to tell people that they have to buy the particular health insurance specified by the federal government.

A bit of retrenchment

There was consternation in 1995 when the Supreme Court ruled in *United States v. Lopez* that carrying a gun near a school was not interstate commerce. That conclusion might seem like common sense to many, but the close 5–4 decision sparked outrage when the phrase "interstate commerce" failed to work its magic in justifying an expansion of the federal government's power.

The 1995 case involved a federal law forbidding anyone to carry a gun near a school. The states all had the right to pass such laws, and most did, but the issue was whether the federal government could pass such a bill under its power to regulate interstate commerce.

The underlying argument of the government was similar to that in *Wickard v. Filburn*: school violence can affect education, which can affect productivity, which can affect interstate commerce. You might call that a stretch.

But not for long

It is helpful that in this case the Court held that there is no connection between firearms being carried near a school and interstate commerce, but it by no means undid the practice of expansive interpretation of the commerce clause by the federal government.

The weed is never local

In 2004, California residents who claimed to suffer from a variety of medical conditions sought to avail themselves of medical marijuana under the terms of California's Compassionate Use Act. After an investigation, county officials concluded that one smoker's use of marijuana was entirely lawful under California law.

The lead plaintiff was Angel Raich of Oakland, who claimed she used marijuana to keep herself alive. She and her doctor claimed to have tried dozens of prescription medicines for her numerous medical conditions and said that she was allergic to most of them. Her doctor declared under oath that Raich's life was at stake if she could not continue to use marijuana. Another plaintiff, Diane Monson, suffered from chronic pain from a car accident a decade before the case. She used marijuana to relieve the pain and muscle spasms around her spine.

Nevertheless, federal agents seized and destroyed all six of her cannabis plants. The pot users brought an action against the Attorney General of the United States and the head of the DEA seeking injunctive and declaratory relief prohibiting the enforcement of the federal Controlled Substances Act (CSA).

The case was taken up at the Supreme Court as *Gonzales v. Raich* in 2005. The issue was whether Congress, under the commerce clause, could forbid the cultivation and use of marijuana in compliance with California law, which use was argued by the users to be strictly in-state and thus not affecting interstate commerce.

As in *Wickard*, the Court held that the regulation of cannabis under the CSA was squarely within Congress's commerce power because the production of marijuana meant for home consumption had a substantial effect on supply and demand in the national market. Given enforcement difficulties stemming from distinguishing between marijuana cultivated locally and marijuana grown elsewhere and concerns about diversion into illicit channels, the Court had no problem concluding that Congress had a rational basis for believing that failure to regulate the intrastate manufacture and possession of marijuana would leave a gaping hole in the CSA. So, the Court concluded that Congress was acting well within its authority under the commerce clause.

The ObamaCare "tax"

Even good arguments against the excessive power over anything remotely related to commerce that *Wickard* allowed still carry little weight in the courts. Liberty University (Lynchburg, Virginia) and two individuals submitted a petition to the Supreme Court arguing for taking a 2011 case from an appeals court to remove the ObamaCare penalty for not buying health insurance. The Court took the case in 2012 as *National Federation of Independent Businesses v. Sebelius.* The four liberal justices made the argument that the penalty was constitutional based on the commerce clause (per *Filburn*). In the end, it was Roberts's twisted reasoning that the penalty was somehow a tax that prevailed. Thus, ObamaCare was ruled constitutional. (See Chapter 13.)

Consequences

Wickard v. Filburn is one of the worst examples of judicial activism in our history. The notion that a farmer who grows grain on his own farm for his own use is somehow engaged in "commerce" is absurd. The decision broadened the definition of the word so much that the federal government may regulate practically anything using its authority under the commerce clause. The decision substantially deprecates the concept of enumerated powers and the Ninth- and Tenth-Amendment protections of rights retained by the people.

Since virtually everything affects virtually everything else, however remotely, "interstate commerce" can, by this kind of sophistry, justify almost any expansion of government power.

Thomas Sowell, writing for Townhall.com, gives this example of how the reasoning in *Wickard* could lead to excessive regulation of everyday life:

> For example, take a law that most everybody would agree is valid: that cars have to stop at red lights. Local governments certainly have the right to pass such laws and to punish those who disobey them. No doubt, people who are tired or drowsy are more likely to run through a red light than people who are rested and alert. But does that mean that local governments should have the power to order people when to go to bed and when to get up because their tiredness can have an effect on the likelihood of their driving through a red light?

The power to regulate based on the indirect effects of any number of human actions remains a grave threat to freedom.

Solutions

The misuse of the commerce clause has become so entrenched that only a constitutional amendment can undo the damage. Randy Barnett of the Cato Institute has proposed the following:

> *The power of Congress to make all laws that are necessary and proper to regulate commerce among the several states, or with foreign nations, shall not be construed to include the power to regulate or prohibit any activity that is confined within a single state regardless of its effects outside*

> *the state, whether it employs instrumentalities therefrom, or whether its regulation or prohibition is part of a comprehensive regulatory scheme; but Congress shall have the power to regulate harmful emissions between one state and another, and to define and provide for punishment of offenses constituting acts of war or violent insurrection against the United States.*

Perhaps this could be one of the amendments coming out of a convention called by the states to consider amendments to the Constitution, as described in Article V. The organization Convention of States is promoting this cause.

W5-AA https://conventionofstates.com.

Follow-up

Most of Filburn's land was sold in 1966 for the development of a residential area and a shopping mall. A street on the property was named Filbrun Lane in his honor (he changed the spelling of his last name after losing the Supreme Court case). Roscoe pursued other interests, including buying a bookshop in nearby Brookville, which he managed with his wife, Virginia. They had two children, neither of whom became farmers. Roscoe himself continued to farm until his death at age 85 in 1987.

For further reading

The Federalist Society has produced a video explaining this

decision and its implications:

W5-AB https://www.youtube.com/watch?v=rS4NRHU23cE

The Filburn Foundation is a nonprofit organization that seeks to bring attention to the damage done to liberty by this case. Among its resources are the full text of petitions for a writ of *certiorari* and Court rulings.

W5-AC http://www.thefilburnfoundation.com/

This 2011 Atlas Society (inspired by author Ayan Rand) blog entry is an analysis of the California medical marijuana case:

W5-AD https://atlassociety.org/commentary/commentary-blog/4643-medical-marijuana-and-the-law-reefer-madness-meets-wickard-v-filburn-

6~*Everson v. Board of Education* (1947)

Our excellent Constitution . . . has not placed our religious rights under the power of any public functionary. —Thomas Jefferson, Letter to the Methodist Episcopal Church, 1808

Sometimes it is not the actual decision in a Supreme Court case that creates problems down the road; instead, certain phrases in the *obiter dicta* at the end of opinions are taken as gospel by justices deciding other cases. That happened in the 1982 ruling *Plyler v. Doe*, discussed in the chapter on *U.S. v. Wong Kim Ark,* which had the eventual effect of adversely changing immigration practices without a change in the law. A similar invitation was set for later bad rulings in the commentary in *Everson v. Board of Education.*

Right decision, dangerous *dicta*

In *Everson v. Board of Education*, the issue was whether the state of New Jersey could reimburse parents for the cost of public transportation used to get their children to school, whether public or private. That most of the private schools were parochial (Catholic) schools bothered a New Jersey taxpayer, who viewed this arrangement as a violation of the First Amendment's establishment clause and the Fourteenth Amendment's due process clause.

The majority, in a decision written by Justice Hugo Black, concluded that these reimbursements were "separate and so indisputably marked off from the religious function" that they did not violate the Constitution. But both affirming and dissenting justices were emphatic that the Constitution required a strong separation between government and religion. Their commentary led to a series of court decisions that effected repression of religious sentiments in the public sphere, way beyond what history shows were the intentions of the writers of the First Amendment. The decision was also the first Supreme Court case incorporating the establishment clause of the First Amendment as binding upon the states through the due process clause of the Fourteenth Amendment.

Hugo Lafayette Black was a pro–New-Deal senator when Franklin Roosevelt chose his first nominee to the Supreme Court, his court-packing scheme having failed. It is not known whether Roosevelt knew that Black had entered the Senate with the backing of the Alabama Ku Klux Klan, then a significant influence in the Democrat party. He had not consulted with any of his usual advisers, but he thought that the appointment of a senator (a first) would surely be confirmed by the Senate and that Black, once on the bench, would defend Roosevelt's often-challenged expansion of government. Black, on the Court until he died in 1971, almost always ruled as Roosevelt had hoped.

Jefferson's wall

The damage came from a misunderstanding of Jefferson's phrase "wall of separation between church and state" in his reply to a letter from the Danbury (Connecticut) Baptists Association. Its leaders were concerned about possible interference with their right to worship in their style from the established majority Congregational and Anglican churches. So, the "wall" analogy was not to limit religious activities in the public sphere but to assure the minority Baptists that the federal government did not have the power to interfere with or limit those expressions. The wall analogy is nowhere in the U.S. Constitution, but, unfortunately, the judiciary at all levels has since embraced this figurative phrase as if it were a rule of constitutional law and the organizing basis of church–state jurisprudence.

Black's wall in subsequent cases

It didn't take long for *Everson* to do damage. The next year in *McCollum v. Board of Education*, the Court leaned on *Everson* to further the objective of an atheist parent, abolishing a voluntary program of religious education by visiting religious teachers in the schools of a New Jersey school district. The school system required written permission for a child to participate and had no involvement in content. So, while the plaintiff's child was not in any way compelled to participate, the plaintiff secured through the Court the mandate that no other students could either, even if their parents wanted them to.

Justice Stanley Reed in his dissent noted, "A rule of law should not be drawn from a figure of speech." But in the seven decades since this landmark ruling, the "wall of separation" has become the foundation of the premise that the First Amendment separated religion and the civil state.

Since *McCollum* was based on a text not in the Constitution, it is an example of judicial activism. The majority was obviously unaware of the many instances of the writer of the "wall" comment supporting religious life and expression while president.

The trope's continuing influence can be seen in Justice John Paul Stevens's warning in his dissent in a 2002 case (*Zelman v. Simmons-Harris*) that our democracy is threatened "whenever we remove a brick from the wall that was designed to separate religion and government."

But the wall that Black built still separates religion and civil government at all levels—federal, state, and local—and, thus, turned the First Amendment upside down. Black's wall restricts religion's ability to influence public life. All too often, the wall of separation is used to silence and limit the reach of religious expressions in public life, but it is rarely used to prohibit the civil state's meddling in and restraint of religious expression.

What was intended

Throughout his public career, Jefferson pursued policies that do not comport with the "high and impregnable" wall the Supreme Court has erroneously attributed to him. For example, he endorsed the use of federal funds to support Christian missionaries working among the Indians to build churches. But many courts and commentators would have us believe that Jefferson routinely pursued policies that violated his "wall of separation."

Jefferson's wall was erected between the national and state governments on matters concerning religion. (Think federalism here.) While Jefferson's wall expressly separated the institutions of church and state, Black's wall, more expansively, separates religion and all civil government.

The pertinent section of the First Amendment said only that the federal government could not establish a church and that it would not interfere with the exercise of religion. As the late Antonin Scalia observed, in the first decades of the republic, the establishment clause was understood to mean that the people were free from having a particular denomination endorsed by the federal government. But the clause has come to mean freedom from encountering any religious expression in the public space.

Even if we include state governments in these prohibitions, there remains some latitude when properly observing the amendment's limited scope for some acknowledgment of a Creator in the public sphere, so long as such expression is in accord with the sentiments of the concerned public in the aggregate and does not promote a particular denomination.

Consequences

That an expression of thanks to a supreme being by a citizen on a public occasion could be an attack on our religiously neutral system of government or social order is not only preposterous but misses the point that such expressions from time to time in venues other than churches might be conducive to social comity and cohesion. This tolerance is especially appropriate in a society whose vast majority adheres to the idea of a supreme being, even if most no longer regularly attend religious services. And the expressions in the early years of the leaders who formed our new nation frequently and unhesitatingly included religious sentiments in reference to educational activities. George Washington deemed faith an indispensable support for social order and political prosperity and wrote in a

1789 letter to the Synod of the Dutch Reform Church:

> While just government protects all in their religious rights, true religion affords to government its surest support.

ACLU attacks

In the years since *Everson*, hardly a month goes by without a lawsuit against a governmental actor objecting to a public expression of a sentiment relating to a supreme being. The American Civil Liberties Union (ACLU) and its allies continue to use the wall meme to silence communities of faith and people who seek to participate in the public marketplace of ideas armed with ideas informed by spiritual values. Much stress, time, and money have been spent on these suits, which usually result in a verdict in favor of the plaintiff. A subtle result of the misreading of the First Amendment's religions clause might be a lessening of interest in and respect for a power higher than human and the benefits both to individuals and the public in the aggregate of an occasional reminder of that power or how fundamental natural law might helpfully guide a discussion on public policy.

Voiding of values in civic life

Today, the wall is a strict separationist dogma intolerant of religious influences in the public square. Federal and state courts have used the "wall of separation" regime to justify censoring private religious expression (such as Christmas crèches) in the public sphere, stripping public spaces of religious symbols (such as crosses), denying public benefits (such as education vouchers) for religious entities, and excluding religious citizens and organizations (such as faith-based social welfare agencies) from full participation in civic life on the same terms as their secular counterparts.

An example of the last is the disqualification of faith-based adoption agencies who refuse for plausible reasons to place children in homes of homosexual couples. This 2019 Michigan settlement in a suit brought by the state ACLU against the state attorney general is an example:

W6-AA https://www.detroitnews.com/story/news/local/michigan/2019/03/22/nessel-settlement-bans-agencies-barring-same-sex-adoptions/3245275002/

The coercive and systematic removal of religion from public life is contrary to our cultural traditions, especially when it effects a callous indifference to religion. In such efforts, fundamental notions of freedom of religious exercise, expression, and association that one would expect in a democratic and pluralistic society are offended.

The threatening Peace Cross

An example is the attack on a cross built by the American Legion in 1925 on private land in Bladensburg, Maryland, to commemorate forty-nine WWI dead (most of whom were Christian). The cross mirrors crosses found on burial plots of military dead in numerous locations in the United States and abroad. It has become known as the Peace Cross. The land and cross were donated to a public park planning commission in 1861, which has since overseen maintenance, including lighting, to minimize hazards to nearby traffic on either side of what is now a median.

In early 2019 the Court heard an appeal from the American Legion following a lower appellate court decision finding that the cross excessively entangled the government and religion per the usual "wall" argument, as argued by the atheist American Humanist Association. This article in *Stars and Stripes* describes the issue:

W6-AB https://www.stripes.com/supreme-court-is-peace-cross-a-war-memorial-or-a-christian-symbol-1.570644

In June that year, the Court ruled in favor of the Legion, but very narrowly, so the public-square issue is still circumscribed.

Constitutional confusion

Several earlier Court cases, such as *Lemon v. Kurtzman* (1970):

W6-AC https://www.oyez.org/cases/1970/89

and *Town of Greece v. Galloway* (2013):

W6-AD https://www.oyez.org/cases/2013/12-696

have allowed for much confusion about what is or is not "constitutional" about public displays that might have a religious inspiration. Decisions that allow for the continued existence of memorials such as the Peace Cross would not in any way establish a government religion, and that they might indirectly reflect the free exercise thereof would be a welcome liberation from what has been misguided and unconstitutional supervision of the people through a persistent and exaggerated misreading of the First Amendment.

Solutions

Congress cannot undo bad Supreme Court decisions, but parties being sued based on the premise that Justice Black's strict separation wall prohibits their actions should contest unreasonable restrictions by appropriate appeals, particularly in times when the Court majority appears to be of a strict-construction, original-intent frame of mind. Maybe a ruling will remove a few bricks from Black's wall and free the people to again refer politely to religious sentiments in public life. When such a case is accepted for argument, consider writing a persuasive letter to each justice in support of a decision that will lessen the unconstitutional Court-created restrictions on religious expression in the public space. The address for letters is:

Hon. [name]
Supreme Court of the United States
1 First Street NE, Washington, DC 20543

For further reading

Original Intent: The Courts, the Constitution, and Religion by David Barton; 1996, Wall BuildersPress:

W6-AE https://shop.wallbuilders.com/books

A Matter of Interpretation: Federal Courts and the Law by Antonin Scalia; 1997, Princeton University Press:

W6-AF https://press.princeton.edu/titles/10859.html

Thomas Jefferson and the Wall of Separation Between Church and States by Daniel Dreisbach; 2002, New York University Press:

W6-AG https://nyupress.org/9780814719367/thomas-jefferson-and-the-wall-of-separation-between-church-and-state/

Separation of Church and State by Philip Hamburger; 2002, Harvard University Press:

W6-AH https://www.hup.harvard.edu/catalog.php?isbn=9780674013742

Separation of Church and State: What the Founders Meant by David Barton; 2007, WallBuilders Press

W6-AI https://shop.wallbuilders.com/separation-of-church-state-what-the-founders-meant-book

Article: "How to respond to 'Separation of Church and State'" by WallBuilders

W6-AJ https://wallbuilders.com/respond-separation-church-state/

7~*Berman v. Parker* (1954) and *Kelo v. City of New London* (2005)

Ultimately property rights and personal rights are the same thing. —Calvin Coolidge

The names of most Supreme Court cases are not well known, but one that is, *Kelo v. City of New London,* is best considered as a follow-on to two earlier eminent domain decisions that are not well known. The Fifth Amendment contains a section that acknowledges that governments might have good reason to take private property for a public purpose: "No person shall . . . be deprived of life, liberty, or property, without due process of law; nor shall private property be taken for public use, without just compensation." Public use was long understood to mean things such as building a new highway or other facility for use by the general public.

A taking in D.C.

But in the mid-twentieth century, a trend began to expand justifications for takings. This expansion started with litigation over a redevelopment plan in Washington, D.C. Congress, acting as the local legislature for the District of Columbia, passed legislation in 1945 enabling the D.C. planning commission to develop a comprehensive redevelopment plan. The primary purpose was to rid the District of Columbia of blighted property and slums. To achieve such ends, the act allowed for the acquisition and assembly of property in the area using eminent domain. Once the property was acquired, the land could be transferred to both public and private agencies. The Act was comprehensive, as it was concerned with modernizing the urban environment as well as with clearing slums.

Target: southwest Washington, D.C.

The first project under the Act was in southwest Washington, D.C. In 1950, a comprehensive plan for the area was published, and soon afterward, the owners (publicly known only as "Berman et al.") of a department store in the target zone brought suit to challenge the constitutionality of the taking of their property. In *Berman v. Parker* the plaintiffs argued that this property was not slum housing and that it could not be taken to be redeveloped for private use simply to make the community more attractive overall. The owners also argued that taking the land under eminent domain and giving it to redevelopers amounted to "a taking from one businessman for the benefit of another businessman" and did not constitute a public use, thus violating the Fifth Amendment's eminent domain clause.

A special three-panel district court heard this challenge to the constitutionality of the District of Columbia Redevelopment Act. The critical issue was the ability and scope of the government to take and transfer private property to private developers as part of a project to clear blight. The D.C. Circuit Court found no problem with the government using eminent domain to remove blighted structures because this effort could be seen as the abatement of a public nuisance.

The lead judge read the Redevelopment Act very narrowly

and found that non-blighted property could be taken so long as the taking could be tied to the prevention of blight and granted the government's motion to dismiss. The Berman side appealed.

Policy over process

The Supreme Court unanimously decided in favor of the Planning Commission. The justices took on a policy role and argued that the problem of large-scale blight needed to be addressed with a massive integrated redevelopment plan. Justice William O. Douglas wrote in his opinion, "If owner after owner were permitted to resist these redevelopment programs on the grounds that his particular property was not being used against the public interest, integrated plans for redevelopment would suffer greatly." As the Planning Commission had made detailed plans and taken extensive surveys of the area in question, the Court argued for judicial restraint.

Douglas wrote, "In the present case, the Congress and its authorized agencies have made determinations that take into account a wide variety of values. It is not for us to reappraise them." The Court stated that there is nothing in the Fifth Amendment that prohibits the District of Columbia from deciding that the capital should be "beautiful as well as sanitary." As the object of cleaning up the area was said to be under the authority of Congress, it followed, according to the Court, that eminent domain was an acceptable way to accomplish this object.

Public use becomes a public purpose

Douglas addressed the issue presented by the landowners of "a taking from one businessman for the benefit of another businessman" by saying that a legitimate public purpose had been established by Congress in creating the entire redevelopment plan; i.e., the objective of the taking was to eliminate slums on an area-wide basis. The Court found that though specific parcels of land may not have been blighted, their taking was necessary for the functioning of the redevelopment plan as a whole. Justice Douglas took an expansive view of "public use" as including "public purpose" based on physical, aesthetic, and monetary benefits. He further stated that the purpose of the redevelopment plan was to address the broader blight issues in the area to prevent the neighborhood from reverting to blighted conditions.

The Court was not interested in addressing the specifics of the plan, saying that "once the question of the public purpose has been decided, the amount and character of the land to be taken for a particular tract to complete the integrated plan rests in the discretion of the legislative branch."

So, the Court concluded that the District of Columbia Redevelopment Land Agency could acquire full title and dispense with the property as it wished, recognizing that the rights afforded a citizen by the Fifth Amendment are satisfied by payment of just compensation. *Berman* determined the legislature's police power broadly and clearly indicated that the Court would not tolerate federal courts replacing the vision of the legislature with its own with respect to how the public interest would be served.

Wholesale land condemnation in Hawaii

The *Berman* Court's deference to a legislative determination that involved interpretation of the public use clause was followed in 1984 by an expanded application of this clause in *Hawaii Housing Authority v. Midkiff et al.* By the mid-1960s, the Hawaii state legislature discovered that only twenty-two individuals owned more than 70% of the fee-simple titles on the Island of Oahu. Believing skewed land prices resulting from concentrated land ownership were harmful to the public, the Hawaiian legislature instituted a plan to compel large landowners to break up their estates.

To minimize the tax consequences for landowners, the legislature created a mechanism by which it would condemn property and transfer ownership to the property's tenants, provided the tenants compensated the landowner. Once a hearing was held and it was determined that the use of eminent domain would achieve a legitimate "public purpose," the land was acquired through either condemnation hearings or negotiations between lessor and lessee.

Police powers promoted

In April of 1977, negotiations between a tenant and one of the landholders, Frank Midkiff, failed, resulting in the initiation of condemnation proceedings against Midkiff's property. Midkiff challenged the Hawaii legislature's plan, arguing that it violated the public use clause of the Fifth Amendment.

The district court determined that the purpose of the legislation was within the scope of the state's police power and that the means to accomplish the end were not arbitrary or capricious. The Court of Appeals for the Ninth Circuit reversed, holding that the legislation was "a naked attempt on the part of Hawaii to take the private property of A and transfer it to B solely for B's private use and benefit."

The Supreme Court, disagreeing with the Ninth Circuit, reversed. The Court again required the purpose to be within the "police power" of the state and applied the holding of *Berman*, declaring the question of the proper scope of "public use" to be a narrow one.

However, the Court seemed to expand the holding of *Berman.* by declaring that "the 'public use' requirement is coterminous with the scope of a sovereign's police power."

Recognizing the states' traditional role of providing relief from the social and economic effects of a monopoly, the Court concluded that this effort to regulate land monopolies was within the bounds of Hawaii's police power. Therefore, despite the reality that eminent domain was being used to transfer land ownership from one private citizen to another, the Court concluded that the Fifth Amendment was not being violated. As in *Berman*, the Court held that if the state's purpose is legitimate and the means are not irrational, federal courts should not replace a legislature's judgment with their own.

So, the Court determined that because using eminent domain to make land ownership more diffuse was not an irrational way to address the legitimate public purpose identified by the Hawaii legislature, the plan did not violate the public use clause of the Fifth Amendment.

Following the *Midkiff* decision, housing prices on Oahu doubled in about five years. Many of the homes in the taking area were bought up by Japanese investors who replaced them with expensive luxury homes.

Public purpose preempts private ownership in New London

Berman and *Midkiff* were reexamined in the 2005 Supreme Court decision *Susette Kelo et al. v. City of New London*, in which the Court extended the *Berman* ruling to allow takings of unblighted private property solely for the economic benefit of the condemning city. The case arose in the context of condemnation by the City of New London, Connecticut, of privately owned real property so it could be used as part of a "comprehensive redevelopment plan."

The owners, including lead plaintiff Susette Kelo, sued the city in a Connecticut court, arguing that the city had misused its eminent domain power. Kelo had moved to New London from northern Maine when she was seven. Her mother got a job as a waitress and sent Kelo and her siblings to local Catholic schools. She married, had five sons, got divorced, but waited until the youngest left high school to pursue a degree in nursing and was working part-time as a paramedic.

One day, she was called to Fort Trumbull to assess a crew member on a ship. The patient did not have to be transported. On her way back from the water, Kelo came across a dilapidated cottage for sale. It needed extensive work, but she was taken by the location and the view. Later, she went with a real estate agent to look at the property. She made an offer and bought the house.

Kelo began to renovate her house, including painting it salmon pink, her favorite color. During this time, she met a stonemason who soon became her husband. He did much of the exterior work on the house, and together they settled in.

In late 2000, the Kelos were notified that they would have to leave their house because it was being taken pursuant to eminent domain. Kelo and others filed suit to challenge the taking.

One night in late 2002, Kelo was working in a hospital emergency room when a man critically hurt in a car accident was rushed in by ambulance. It was only after working alongside the rest of the medical staff for some time that Kelo realized the man was her husband. For two weeks, he remained in a coma, and he was hospitalized for two months.

While her husband was at home recovering from his disabling brain injury, her neighbors helped care for him. Kelo was also busy preparing her legal case with her fellow plaintiffs. They argued that economic development, the stated purpose of the taking and subsequent transfer of land to the New London Development Corporation, did not qualify as a public use under the Fifth Amendment. The Supreme Court of Connecticut decided in favor of New London, so the plaintiffs appealed to the Supreme Court.

Public use loses to public purpose

The Supreme Court granted *certiorari* to consider questions raised in the *Berman* and *Midkiff* cases regarding whether a "public purpose" constitutes a "public use" for purposes of the Fifth Amendment's takings clause. Specifically, does the Fifth Amendment, applicable to the states through the due process clause of the Fourteenth Amendment, protect landowners from a taking for economic development (rather than, as in *Berman*, the elimination of slums and blight)?

In June 2005, the Court ruled 5–4 in favor of the City of New London. Justice Stevens wrote the majority opinion, joined by

Justices Anthony Kennedy, David Souter, Ruth Bader Ginsburg, and Stephen Breyer. Justice Kennedy wrote a separate opinion setting out a more detailed standard for judicial review of economic development takings than that found in Stevens's majority opinion. Justice Kennedy's opinion contributed to the Court's trend of turning minimum scrutiny—the idea that government policy need bear only a rational relation to a legitimate government purpose—into a fact-based test.

Kelo did not make entirely new law concerning eminent domain. Although the decision was controversial, it was not, as we have seen in *Berman* and *Midkiff*, the first time "public use" had been interpreted by the Supreme Court as being a "public purpose." As Justice Stevens wrote in the majority opinion, the "Court long ago rejected any literal requirement that condemned property be put into use for the general public."

However, in those earlier cases, the Court justified the use of eminent domain on the basis of the elimination of social harms such as barriers to efficient exploitation of agricultural and mineral-bearing land, removal of slums, and large-scale title misallocation. None of these factors were present in *Kelo*; the city merely wanted to increase its tax revenues by attracting a wealthier population in place of the lower-middle-class homeowners in the redevelopment project area.

Considering the damage to natural rights concerning property, it is only small comfort that there were four dissenters. The principal dissent by Justice O'Connor, joined by Chief Justice Rehnquist and Justices Scalia and Thomas, suggested that the use of this taking power in a reverse Robin Hood fashion—take from the poor, give to the rich—would become the norm, not the exception.

In a separate dissent, the usually constitutional Justice Thomas stated:

> Today's decision is simply the latest in a string of our cases construing the public use clause to be a virtual nullity, without the slightest nod to its original meaning. In my view, the public use clause, originally understood, is a meaningful limit on the government's eminent domain power. Our cases have strayed from the clause's original meaning, and I would reconsider them. Any property may now be taken for the benefit of another private party, but the fallout from this decision will not be random. The beneficiaries are likely to be those citizens with disproportionate influence and power in the political process, including large corporations and development firms. . . Though citizens are safe from the government in their homes, their homes are not safe from the government.

Despite the dissent, the decision did very little to limit the use of eminent domain as it applies to the Fifth Amendment. The majority recognized the expanded police power of the state, holding that as long as the state could show that the eminent domain power was being used to protect the public health, safety, and welfare, the Court could continue its refusal to question the wisdom of the legislature regarding the means chosen to accomplish such ends. The *Kelo* decision, like *Berman* and *Midkiff*, illustrated that while the Court may look cursorily into the purpose behind a legislature's use of eminent domain, it will refrain from any real scrutiny regarding the legislature's purpose or the mechanism the legislature has chosen to achieve that purpose.

Subsequent developments

Following the decision, many of the plaintiffs expressed an intent to find other means by which they could continue contesting the seizure of their homes. Soon after the ruling, city officials announced plans to charge residents for back rent for the five years since condemnation procedures were instituted. The city contended that the residents had been on city property for those five years and owed tens of thousands of dollars of rent. In June 2006, Governor M. Jodi Rell intervened with New London city officials, proposing that the homeowners involved in the suit be deeded property in the Fort Trumbull neighborhood so they could keep their homes.

The controversy was eventually settled when the city paid substantial additional compensation to the homeowners and agreed to move Kelo's home to a new location. The land was never deeded back to the original homeowners, most of whom had left New London. Three years after the case was decided, the Kelo house was relocated to a site close to downtown New London by The Institute for Justice and was dedicated as a foundation. Susette Kelo moved to a different part of Connecticut.

W7-AA http://www.ij.org/susette-kelos-little-pink-house-finds-a-new-foundation-2

Despite repeated efforts, the redeveloper (who stood to get a 91-acre waterfront tract of land for $1 per year) was unable to obtain financing and abandoned the redevelopment project. At the beginning of 2010, the original Kelo property was a vacant lot, generating no tax revenue for the city. In the aftermath of

2011's Hurricane Irene, the by-then-closed redevelopment area was used as a dump for storm debris. As of this writing, it was still vacant, except for feral cats. This 2018 *Reason* article sums up the irony:

W7-AB https://reason.com/2018/05/25/give-susette-kelo-back-her-land/

Consequences

The *Kelo* decision was greeted by widespread outrage from the public and resulted in presidential, congressional, and state efforts to change eminent domain laws.

Public

Public reaction to the decision was highly unfavorable. Much of the public viewed the outcome as a gross violation of rights concerning property and as a misinterpretation of the Fifth Amendment, the consequence of which would be to benefit large corporations at the expense of individual homeowners and local communities. Some in the legal profession construed the public's outrage as being directed at the broad moral principles of the outcome rather than at the interpretation of legal principles involved in the case.

Opposition to the ruling was widespread, coming from varied groups such as AARP, the NAACP, and the Libertarian Party as well as the Institute for Justice. Many owners of family farms also disapproved of the ruling, which they saw as an avenue by which cities could seize their land for private developments. The grassroots lobbying group American Conservative Union described the decision as judicial activism, as did numerous blogs, such as this one by the Cato Institute:

W7-AC https://www.cato.org/publications/commentary/grasping-hand-kelo-v-city-new-london-limits-eminent-domain

One result is that many states changed their eminent domain laws. Before the *Kelo* ruling, only eight states expressly prohibited the use of eminent domain for economic development except to eliminate blight. Since the decision, forty-four states have amended their eminent domain laws (although some of these changes were cosmetic).

The *Kelo* disaster eventually cost the taxpayers tens of millions of dollars and gave them nothing to show for it. The "carefully vetted" municipal plans that formed the basis for the Supreme Court's decision proved to be illusory. Eventually, the City of New London extended an apology to Susette Kelo and her neighbors, and so did one of the Connecticut Supreme Court justices who voted for the city.

Presidential

On the first anniversary of the original decision, President George W. Bush issued an executive order instructing the federal government to restrict the use of eminent domain; however, since eminent domain is often exercised by local and state governments, this presidential order may have little overall effect.

Congressional

In the aftermath of *Kelo,* various bills limiting eminent domain have been filed in the House of Representatives. As some small-scale eminent domain condemnations (including notably those in the *Kelo* case) can be local in both decision and funding, it is unclear how much of an effect these bills would have if passed into law.

State

Before *Kelo,* seven states expressly prohibited the use of eminent domain for economic development except to eliminate blight: Arkansas, Florida, Kansas, Kentucky, Maine, New Hampshire, South Carolina, and Washington. Following *Kelo*, forty-four states have enacted some reform legislation in response. Of those, twenty-two enacted laws that severely restricted the takings allowed by the *Kelo* decision. The rest passed laws that placed some limits on the power of municipalities to use eminent domain for economic development.

However, cases of eminent domain abuse continue. In 2014, the Jackson, Mississippi, suburb of Ridgeland used its property code to try to get rid of older apartment complexes to reduce rental properties. The town rezoned sections of Southeast Ridgeland from multifamily to mixed-use, forcing many buildings into noncompliance, including some with ongoing improvements. The *Mississippi Business Journal* reported:

W7-AD http://msbusiness.com/2014/09/whats-behind-plan-apartment-zoning-ridgeland-targets-minorities-lawsuit-says

In 2015, Dallas rezoned a neighborhood to spur its gentrification. An auto repair shop opened in 1986 and built over the years by a formerly penniless immigrant from Kenya, Hinga Mbogo, was ordered to cease business by a specified year. His appeal was turned down in 2016 by the Dallas City Council and the shop was forced to move. The Institute for Justice entered an appearance on his behalf to fight for his effort to return to his former, now empty, lot on Ross Avenue, which the City Council wanted to transform into a gateway to the arts district.

W7-AE https://ij.org/press-release/hingas-automotive-will-take-its-case-to-the-texas-supreme-court/

Solutions

The primary divergence from past precedent in these cases is the growing dissent. While *Berman* and *Midkiff* were unanimous decisions, *Kelo* was decided by a split Court, with the author of the *Midkiff* decision leading the charge for the dissent. However, the dissent did not question the means by which the legislature was attempting to achieve its ends; rather, Justice O'Connor questioned the ultimate purpose or end desired by the legislature. While *Kelo* upheld *Berman* and *Midkiff*, the dissents signaled a future in which the state might face a greater burden in showing that its use of eminent domain to acquire private land for subsequent private use satisfies the public use clause of the Fifth Amendment.

That's more of a hope than a certainty. So, while there is no clear national course of public action on this subject, citizens of states that have not clarified their eminent domain policies to prevent a *Kelo* scenario or that have done so only weakly should let their state legislators know how they feel. Legislatures could require heightened scrutiny of costs and benefits and enact higher-compensation rules, such as a value-plus-25% rule for compensation, which would reduce eminent domain initiatives and compensate owners for the disruption in their lives. Even more fundamental, they could limit by statute the purposes permitted for takings. It might be necessary to prohibit blight-based takings, as governments might choose to assert this justification when the real one is economic development.

For further reading

Little Pink House by Jeff Benedict; 2009, Hachette. A film of the same name was released in 2015:

W7-AF https://www.facebook.com/littlepinkhousemovie

The Grasping Hand by Ilya Somin; 2015, University of Chicago Press, 2015:

W7-AG https://press.uchicago.edu/ucp/books/author/S/I/au8304634.html

Video by Jeff Benedict at

W7-AH https://www.youtube.com/watch?v=SZiyzwNhmj0

The Institute for Justice fights many battles for individual freedom and property rights:

W7-AI https://www.ij.org/issues/private-property

8~*Bennis v. Michigan* (1996)

. . . nor shall any State deprive any person of life, liberty, or property, without due process of law . . .
—Fourteenth Amendment

Civil asset forfeiture is the practice of the state taking someone's property, based on suspicion that the property has been used for wrongdoing without having to charge them with a crime. It has its origins in British maritime law. The British (like the new United States) experienced hostile engagements with pirates along the Barbary Coast. When the pirates were apprehended and their ships brought to London, British courts had difficulty deciding what to do with these ships. The ships' owners were outside the jurisdiction of British law—so the courts couldn't try and convict them—but neither would they send the vessels back to them only to have them returned to the seas with fresh pirate crews. So parliament passed a law allowing the courts to charge the property itself with the crime if, and only if, the property's owner was outside the jurisdiction of British law.

Civil asset forfeiture, in this minimal form, was part of American law from the beginning. That is, when the culprits were physically out of reach of authorities or the jurisdiction of the country's courts, the legal fiction that their property could be charged with wrongdoing at a civil trial could be created. And when they were found liable for wrongdoing, such properties (and only those properties) were seized.

But this limited concept of forfeiture began to expand. In the late nineteenth century, when alcohol was prohibited in some American states, law enforcers began using civil asset forfeiture to confiscate the property of people suspected of producing and selling alcohol. This expanded view of seizure allowed them to circumvent due process, as American law guarantees due process rights (such as the right to a trial by jury, the right to an attorney, the presumption of innocence, etc.) only to real persons. More recently, suspected drug dealing has replaced alcohol as a justification for forfeiture, especially after the passage of the Comprehensive Crime Control Act of 1984, which outlined provisions for forfeiture operations.

Abuses abound

The Comprehensive Crime Control Act permits local and federal law enforcement agencies to divvy up seized cash and other assets. The threshold for suspicion of criminal involvement is absurdly low and encourages law enforcement agencies to abuse the power of civil forfeiture. Many innocent citizens have had their property seized.

The Scott killing

A particularly egregious pre-*Bennis* example was the killing of Donald Scott in his home on his 250-acre Ventura County estate near Malibu. On October 2, 1992, a "task force" composed of Los Angeles County deputy sheriffs, DEA agents, and U.S. Park Service officers executed a search warrant on the Scott estate. The warrant was based on information from an informant that marijuana was growing on Scott's land.

The task force arrived at Scott's estate before 9 a.m. They crashed through the door and pushed Scott's wife, Frances

Plante, through the kitchen into the living room. She screamed, "Don't shoot me! Don't kill me!" apparently awakening her husband, who came downstairs brandishing a gun over his head. According to Plante, the officers told him to lower his weapon, and, as he dropped his arm, they shot him to death and left him lying on the floor as they searched the premises. They found no trace of marijuana anywhere on the estate.

When Plante ran to the body, officers hustled her out of the house. Recorded phone conversations show that while the dead or dying millionaire lay in a pool of blood, police used the phone to make calls and answered a call from one of Scott's neighbors, telling the neighbor that Scott was "busy."

It was later discovered that officials from multiple law enforcement agencies had discussed seizing the home. A report of the District Attorney of Ventura County revealed that he determined that property forfeiture was indeed one of the primary motivations for the raid. Scott had rejected repeated overtures by the National Park Service, which probably wanted to buy the property to incorporate it into a scenic corridor in the Santa Monaco Mountains. This article from Forfeiture Endangers American Rights tells the sad story and lists some other accounts of this deadly abuse.

W8-AA http://www.fear.org/scott15.html

A car is deemed criminal

Bennis v. Michigan was a decision by the United States Supreme Court holding that the innocent-owner defense is not constitutionally mandated by Fourteenth Amendment due process in cases of civil forfeiture.

Mrs. Bennis's struggle

Tina Bennis was a joint owner, with her husband, of an automobile in which her husband engaged in sexual activity with a prostitute. In declaring the automobile forfeit as a public nuisance under Michigan's statutory abatement scheme, the trial court permitted no offset for the petitioner's interest, notwithstanding her lack of knowledge of her husband's activity. The Michigan Court of Appeals reversed but was, in turn, reversed by the Michigan Supreme Court, which concluded, among other things, that Michigan's failure to provide an innocent-owner defense was without federal constitutional consequence.

The ruling

On March 4, 1996, in *Bennis v. Michigan*, the United States Supreme Court held that there was nothing wrong with the government forfeiting a woman's car when her husband, without her knowledge or consent, had sex in it with a prostitute. Chief Justice Rehnquist, writing for the five-justice majority, said forfeiture has nothing to do with the owner's culpability. The property was the offending party and consequently it, not its owner, was being punished. Even the usually right Clarence Thomas erred here by joining the majority.

Dissents

Of the four dissenters, Justice Stevens wrote the most cogent dissent. It begins:

> For centuries, prostitutes have been plying their trade on other people's property. Assignations have occurred in palaces, luxury hotels, cruise ships, college dormitories, truck stops, back alleys, and back seats. A profession of this vintage

has provided governments with countless opportunities to use novel weapons to curtail its abuses.

As far as I am aware, however, it was not until 1988 that any State decided to experiment with the punishment of innocent third parties by confiscating property in which, or on which, a single transaction with a prostitute has been consummated. The logic of the Court's analysis would permit the States to exercise virtually unbridled power to confiscate vast amounts of property where professional criminals have engaged in illegal acts.

Other excerpts:

Here . . . the forfeited property bore no necessary connection to the offense committed by the petitioner's husband.

Even judged in isolation, the remedial interest in this forfeiture falls far short of that which we have found present in other cases. Apart from the lack of a sufficient nexus between the petitioner's car and the offense her husband committed, I would reverse because the petitioner is entirely without responsibility for that act. Fundamental fairness prohibits the punishment of innocent people.

The unique facts of this case demonstrate that the petitioner is entitled to the protection of that rule. The subject of this forfeiture was certainly not contraband. It was not acquired with the proceeds of criminal activity and its principal use was entirely legitimate. It was an ordinary car that petitioner's husband used to commute to the steel mill

> where he worked.
>
> The absence of any deterrent value reinforces the punitive nature of this forfeiture law. But petitioner has done nothing that warrants punishment.
>
> I believe the Court errs today by assuming that the power to seize property is virtually unlimited.

The full text of his dissent can be found at

W8-AB https://www.law.cornell.edu/supct/html/94-8729.ZD.html

How the court erred

Rational people understand that the Bennises' car did not drive to the location of the crime on its own, did not pick up the prostitute on its own, and did not involve itself in the activities of concern to law enforcement without assistance.

This case focuses attention on the balance between an individual's property rights and the government's interest in ensuring that crime doesn't pay. Taking ill-gotten property from a criminal is one thing; that's one purpose of forfeiture. But what possible benefit could come from taking Mrs. Bennis's interest in her car and leaving open the possibility of taking the property of people who no one could argue are negligent or guilty of criminal activity?

Tina Bennis argued that the forfeiture of her interest in the automobile violated her due process rights since the state had no legitimate interest in punishing an innocent person. As she had not been convicted of any crime, her property had been taken without due process. In ruling otherwise, the Court ignored the plain text of the Fifth and Fourteenth Amendments.

Further, if personal assets of innocent parties are subject to a snap taking by police, financial institutions may decide to refrain from providing credit and banking services to otherwise eligible individuals. Under this ruling, it could be that whatever "reasonable steps" the lender might take to prevent wrongful use of property would be deemed insufficient or irrelevant. Innocent third parties should not be treated as criminals. Government officials must learn to view situations as if they or their relatives were the third parties, despite the government's financial incentives to act otherwise.

Consequences

This ruling was a wasted opportunity to curb forfeiture abuse and likely emboldened police units already inclined to grab cash or property with no or only slight connection to criminal activity. Because property rights form the basis of a free society, any law that burdens an innocent owner's property or obligates that owner to prove his or her innocence violates both the due process clause of the Fourteenth Amendment and the takings clause of the Fifth Amendment.

Below are some post-*Bennis* instances of law officers grabbing assets, often cash, sometimes vehicles, and even people's houses.

Danger on the road

In 1998 an African American man was pulled over while traveling from Virginia to Delaware, allegedly for having a taillight out. Though he had no firearms and no drugs, he said that he had $3,500 in cash. The officer promptly seized the driver's cash because he looked like a drug dealer to the officer. This episode is one of several stories related in this 2013 *The Nation* article:

W8-AC https://www.thenation.com/article/when-did-serve-protect-become-seize-profit/

Tenaha, Texas has a reputation for aggressively seizing property and cash not connected with any crime from drivers passing through town on their way to and back from a nearby casino in Louisiana. This 2009 *Chicago Tribune* story cites several such cases in the previous two years:

W8-AD https://www.chicagotribune.com/nation-world/chi-texas-profiling_wittmar10-story.html

Business property at risk

In 2009, Tewksbury, Massachusetts motel owner Russ Caswell was informed by federal agents that his motel was being seized because the property had been used during the commission of drug crimes. After three years of court battles and high legal fees, the forfeiture case was ultimately dismissed. Mr. Caswell has since sold the property to a developer. This 2015 *Daily Signal* article describes this massive misuse of asset forfeiture:

W8-AE http://dailysignal.com/2015/05/07/after-having-his-motel-seized-by-the-government-victim-of-civil-asset-forfeiture-reflects-on-his-fight/

In 2010, a father and son driving through New Mexico to Las Vegas were pulled over twice. In Albuquerque, the stop was supported by the presence of an officer with the Department of Homeland Security, who promptly seized the $17,000 in cash noted by the first detailing officer. Again, no drugs. This *Albuquerque Journal* article relates the sorry saga:

W8-AF https://www.abqjournal.com/108562/profiling-for-profit-cops-take-17k-from-father-son.html

Even regular banking for cash-based businesses can trigger federal action. In 2012, the federal government seized $446,000 from the checking account of a small family-owned distribution business that makes frequent large cash deposits of money received from the stores it serves. In 2015, the Obama Justice Department returned the funds to the company, but the firm nearly had to fold. This Institute for Justice press release describes the sinister saga:

W8-AG https://ij.org/case/long-island-forfeiture/

Air and train travel not safe from government grabs

In 2014, an airline passenger admitted to police who had detained him that he had smoked marijuana on the way to the airport, but he had none in his possession at the terminal. He disclosed when asked that he had $11,000 in cash; the officers moved forcefully to take it and arrest him.

In 2015, DEA agents seized $16,000 from an Amtrak traveler without grounds. The DEA's explanation for the seizure: "We don't have to prove that the person is guilty. It's that the money is presumed to be guilty."

More detail about some of the above cases of abuse as well as the Scott killing can be found at this Listverse site:

W8-AH http://listverse.com/2015/06/29/10-egregious-abuses-of-civil-asset-forfeiture/

Some retrenchment develops

In 2015, the Obama Justice Department mostly ended the

property-seizure program in response to complaints from many sources. In March 2017, the Inspector General at Justice issued a report critical of the program:

W8-AI https://oig.justice.gov/reports/2017/e1702.pdf

But this is pared back

Unfortunately, the Trump Justice Department under Jeff Sessions partially reinstated civil asset forfeiture in 2017, citing an increase in violent crime and drug abuse. Excluded are seizures in states that have outlawed such procedures, and seizures can be applied only to violations of federal law. This article in *The Atlantic* describes the slip backward:

W8-AJ https://www.theatlantic.com/politics/archive/2017/07/sessions-forfeiture-justice-department-civil/534168/

There was an effort in the House in 2018 to undo Sessions' reactivation of forfeiture programs, but nothing passed. So, the abuse resumed. In 2019, police in Alabama seized a house and cash after finding $50 worth of marijuana belonging to the owners' son. This *Reason* article describes this serious violation of property rights:

W8-AK https://reason.com/2019/04/12/alabama-cops-raided-their-house-seized-t/

Solutions

Forfeiture policies achieved national scandal status beginning in the early 1990s. Members of the House Judiciary Committee of both parties kept promising to fix those laws, but somehow never quite got around to it. The forfeiture laws are one of the most flagrant constitutional abuses Americans now suffer. But asset forfeiture is one area where liberals and conservatives could agree, as described in this article by the left-leaning ACLU (wait for donation request to close):

W8-AL https://www.aclu.org/blog/washington-markup/there-bi-partisan-agreement-uncivility-civil-asset-forfeiture

and the right-leaning Freedom Works:

W8-AM http://www.freedomworks.org/tag/civil-asset-forfeiture.

2019 rescue of a Land Rover may lead to remediation

Some correction of excessive asset forfeiture may result from a 2019 case, *Timbs v. Indiana*, a case about excessive fines and selective enforcement. When Tyson Timbs pleaded guilty to selling just under $400 worth of heroin, his Land Rover (which cost $42,000) was seized using civil asset forfeiture. Timbs appealed his case, arguing that the seizure of his Land Rover amounted to an excessive fine in violation of the Eighth Amendment because the SUV was worth more than four times the maximum fine for his crimes. He won his appeals in the lower courts. However, the Indiana Supreme Court reversed the appeals court decision, stating there was no Supreme Court precedent involving the excessive fines clause.

But the Supreme Court ruled that the seizure violated the excessive fines clause; this was the first time it referenced this Bill of Rights clause in a decision. The decision provided no guidelines for what is to be considered excessive, but it might at least give pause to police contemplating an asset seizure and encourage legislative reform. The

Constitution Accountability Center has this entry on the case and lists other commentaries on it:

W8-AN
https://www.theusconstitution.org/litigation/timbs-v-indiana/

Reform needed at both state and federal level

Reform is needed at both the state and federal levels. According to the Institute for Justice, only ten states require a conviction for most or all forfeiture actions. And some of those states can get around restrictions by collaborating with federal agents and turn over seized property under an "equitable sharing" program. Often attempts at reform at the state level are met with opposition by law enforcement authorities who do not want to give up a cash cow. New Mexico has made the most progress, as described in this 2018 *Forbes* article:

W8-AO https://www.forbes.com/sites/nick-sibilla/2018/12/19/cops-cant-ignore-new-mexicos-ban-on-civil-forfeiture-court-rules/#6f425d8f6a7d

For further reading and action

Policing for Profit, a report by the Institute for Justice, updated as necessary:

W8-AP http://ij.org/report/policing-for-profit/

A 2014 *Slate* article describes well some abuses by seizures related to marijuana growing:

W8-AQ https://slate.com/news-and-politics/2014/04/equitable-sharing-legalized-marijuana-and-civil-forfeiture-the-scheme-that-allows-local-cops-to-seize-pot-related-assets-and-profit-from-them-even-where-pot-is-legal.html

U.S. Senator Rand Paul (R–Ky.) has been active on this issue:

W8-AR http://dailycaller.com/2015/01/27/rand-paul-tries-to-stop-cops-from-stealing-your-stuff/

The Forfeiture Endangers American Rights Foundation (FEAR) is engaged in this space:

W8-AS http://www.fear.org.

9~*Roe v. Wade* (1973)

[But] by foreclosing all democratic outlet for the deep passions that this issue arouses, by banishing the issue from the political forum that gives all participants, even the losers, the satisfaction of a fair hearing and an honest fight, by continuing the imposition of a rigid national rule instead of allowing for regional differences, the Court merely prolongs and intensifies the anguish. —Justice Antonin Scalia in his dissent

This is the one Supreme Court case that almost every American knows because it was such an overreach of the Court into the sphere of law-making and an attack on state powers and the rights of the people to influence public policy about a complex moral issue. In disallowing many state and federal restrictions on abortion in the United States, *Roe v. Wade* reinvigorated a discussion about what methods the Supreme Court should use in constitutional adjudication, what role religious and moral views should play in the political sphere, and what matters are for the states, not the federal government. And this is the decision that transformed theretofore pro forma hearings on appointments to the Court into major political battles. Recall the hyper-personal and unsubstantiated attacks on nominees Clarence Thomas in 1991 and Brett Kavanaugh in 2019.

The case

In *Roe v. Wade* and a companion case, *Doe v. Bolton*, the Court ruled 7–2 that a right to privacy under the due process clause of the Fourteenth Amendment extends to a woman's decision to have an abortion, but that this right must be balanced against the states' two legitimate interests in regulating abortions: protecting women's health and protecting the potentiality of human life. The majority believed that these state interests become stronger over the course of pregnancy and therefore limited state regulation of abortion to the third trimester of pregnancy.

According to the Court, "the restrictive criminal abortion laws in effect in a majority of States today are of relatively recent vintage." Providing a historical analysis of abortion, Justice Harry Blackmun noted that abortion was "resorted to without scruple" in Greek and Roman times.

Blackmun also recalled restrictive and permissive attitudes toward abortions and laws throughout history, noting the disagreements among leaders of different professions in those eras and the formative laws and cases. In the United States, Connecticut passed the first state statute criminalizing abortion in 1821. Every state had abortion legislation by 1900. In the United States, abortion was sometimes considered a common-law crime.

Background

The plaintiff, Norma Nelson McCorvey, was born in September 1947 to Mary and Olin Nelson. McCorvey ran away from home at one point and, after returning, was sent to reform school. After the family moved to Houston, her parents divorced when she was 13. McCorvey suffered abuse, met and married Elwood McCorvey at age 16, and left Texas for California.

When she returned, pregnant and frightened, her mother took her baby to raise. McCorvey's second child was raised by the father of the baby without her participation. McCorvey initially said that her third pregnancy was the result of rape, but years later she said she had invented the rape story in an attempt to make a stronger case for an abortion. She was referred to lawyers Sarah Weddington and Linda Coffee by an adoption lawyer.

Weddington and Coffee were searching for a woman who wanted an abortion but could not afford one. Her lawyers were not concerned about the rape story because they wanted to establish a right to abortion for all women, not just those who had been raped. They also needed a plaintiff who would remain pregnant and not travel to where abortion was legal because they feared that if their plaintiff obtained an abortion outside of Texas, her case could be considered moot and thrown out. McCorvey agreed to hire them to represent her.

In 1970, Coffee and Weddington filed suit in the United States District Court for the Northern District of Texas on behalf of McCorvey (under the alias "Jane Roe"). Henry Wade was the Dallas County District Attorney who represented the State of Texas, the defendant. McCorvey no longer claimed that her pregnancy was a result of rape.

In June, a three-judge panel of the district court unanimously declared the Texas law unconstitutional, finding that it violated the right to privacy that it believed was found in the Ninth Amendment. Also, the court relied on Justice Arthur Goldberg's concurrence in *Griswold v. Connecticut* (1965), in which the Court found that a law prohibiting the sale and use of contraceptives violated a right to marital privacy (more on *Griswold* under "How the court erred" later in this chapter.) The district court, however, declined to grant an injunction prohibiting enforcement of the law.

At the Supreme Court

Roe v. Wade reached the Supreme Court on appeal in 1970. For various reasons, the case was not fully argued until October 1972. In the interim, Justice Blackmun worked on possible opinions. He spent a week researching the history of abortion at the Mayo Clinic in Minnesota, where he had worked in the 1950s. After the Court heard the second round of arguments, Powell said he would agree with Blackmun's conclusion and suggested that the Court strike down the Texas law on privacy grounds. Justice Byron White was unwilling to sign on to Blackmun's opinion, and Rehnquist had already decided to dissent.

The decision

In January 1973, a 7–2 majority voted in favor of plaintiff "Roe." Burger, Douglas, and Stewart filed concurring opinions, and Justice White filed a dissenting opinion in which Rehnquist joined. The Court deemed abortion a fundamental right under the United States Constitution, thereby subjecting all laws attempting to restrict it to the standard of "strict scrutiny" as opposed to "rational basis."

Right to privacy

The Court declined to adopt the district court's Ninth Amendment rationale and instead asserted that the

> right of privacy, whether it be found in the Fourteenth Amendment's concept of personal liberty and restrictions upon state action, as we feel it is, or, as the district court determined, in the Ninth Amendment's reservation of rights to the people, is broad enough to encompass a woman's decision whether or not to terminate her pregnancy.

Blackmun's majority opinion explicitly rejected a right-to-life argument on behalf of the fetus. The Court instead recognized the right to an abortion as a fundamental right included within the guarantee of personal privacy. As a result, regulations limiting abortion must be justified by a "compelling state interest" and legislative enactments regulating abortion must be narrowly tailored to a compelling interest, triggering strict scrutiny analysis of abortion regulations.

The trimester invention

Blackmun's opinion created a trimester framework with which to balance the "fundamental right" to abortion with the government's two legitimate interests of protecting the mother's health and protecting the "potentiality of human life." The trimester framework addressed when a woman's fundamental right to abortion would be absolute and when the state's interests would become compelling. The Court left the decision to abort in the first trimester completely to the woman and her physician. From approximately the end of the first trimester until fetal viability, the state's interest in protecting the health of the mother would become "compelling." During that time, the state could regulate the abortion procedure if the regulation was "reasonably related to the preservation and protection of maternal health."

At the point of viability, which the Court believed to be in the third trimester, the state's interest in "potential life" would become compelling and the state could regulate abortion to protect potential life. The state could even forbid abortion at that point so long as it made an exception to preserve the life or health of the mother. The Court added that the primary right being protected in *Roe* was that of a physician to practice medicine freely absent a compelling state interest, not women's rights in general.

Justiciability and deception

There were good reasons to question whether the case was arguable. One was standing: could McCorvey assert the rights of other pregnant women? As she did not present an "actual case or controversy" (a grievance and a demand for relief), any opinion issued by the Supreme Court would constitute an advisory opinion, something not within the scope of what federal courts are permitted to do, according to Article III. The function of a court is to remedy actual harm, not to debate policy in hypothetical cases.

Also, McCorvey's appeal could have been considered "moot" because she had already given birth to her child and therefore would not be affected by the ruling. Also compromising the decision is that the federal trial court decision was not considered by an intermediate appellate court, but rather went directly to the Supreme Court.

There was also a good deal of deception involved. Norma McCorvey initially told her lawyers she had been gang-raped, but actually her boyfriend had impregnated her. McCorvey's lawyers led her to believe she could get an abortion if she let them take her case. Given the time needed to move cases through the courts, this was highly unlikely, and McCorvey gave birth to her child and placed it for adoption. Also, McCorvey never appeared in court; she just signed documents presented by her lawyers. None of the above would necessarily be grounds for dismissing the case, but they do diminish its weight.

Dissents

Two justices presented strong dissenting opinions. Byron White wrote:

> I find nothing in the language or history of the Constitution to support the Court's judgment. The Court simply fashions and announces a new constitutional right for pregnant women and, with scarcely any reason or authority for its action, invests that right with sufficient substance to override most existing state abortion statutes. The upshot is that the people and the legislatures of the fifty states are constitutionally disentitled to weigh the relative importance of the continued existence and development of the fetus, on the one hand, against a spectrum of possible impacts on the woman, on the other hand. As an exercise of raw judicial power, the Court perhaps has authority to do what it does today; but, in my view, its judgment is an improvident and extravagant

> exercise of the power of judicial review that the Constitution extends to this Court.

White asserted that the Court "values the convenience of the pregnant mother more than the continued existence and development of the life or potential life that she carries." Though he suggested that he "might agree" with the Court's values and priorities, he saw "no constitutional warrant for imposing such an order of priorities on the people and legislatures of the States." White criticized the Court for involving itself in the issue of abortion by creating "a constitutional barrier to state efforts to protect human life and by investing mothers and doctors with the constitutionally protected right to exterminate it." He would have left this issue, for the most part, "with the people and to the political processes the people have devised to govern their affairs."

William Rehnquist asserted that the Court's historical analysis was flawed:

> To reach its result, the Court necessarily has had to find within the scope of the Fourteenth Amendment a right that was apparently completely unknown to the drafters of the Amendment. As early as 1821, the first state law dealing directly with abortion was enacted by the Connecticut Legislature. By the time of the adoption of the Fourteenth Amendment in 1868, there were at least 36 laws enacted by state or territorial legislatures limiting abortion. While many States have amended or updated their laws, 21 of the laws on the books in 1868 remain in effect today.

Rehnquist concluded, "There apparently was no question concerning the validity of this provision or of any of the other state statutes when the Fourteenth Amendment was adopted." Therefore, in his view, "the drafters did not intend to have the Fourteenth Amendment withdraw from the States the power to legislate with respect to this matter."

The Court's errors

As we have seen, *Roe v. Wade* settled nothing but did divide the country into still-warring camps. It was questionable public policy and badly derived. Let's examine the tortured reasoning that led to it.

A new privacy theory

To understand the reasoning of the majority, one must know about the 1965 case of *Griswold v. Connecticut*. A Hartford Planned Parenthood clinic official, Estelle Griswold, challenged an unenforced law that made it a criminal offense for a married couple to buy contraceptives. In what might have been a scenario set up expressly to challenge and overturn this law, Griswold was convicted of buying contraceptives and fined. That gave her standing to challenge the constitutionality of the statute on appeal—which she did. The Supreme Court struck down the Connecticut law, holding that the Constitution created substantive rights that were so "fundamental to the principles of liberty" that they could not be restricted by government.

The Constitution does not mention contraception or privacy, but the Court declared in Justice Douglas's majority opinion that the other rights in the Constitution contain "penumbra" and "emanations" of implied rights, and the general right to privacy was determined to be one of these rights. The statute prohibiting the use of contraceptives was voided as an infringement of the right of marital privacy.

The Court's reliance on privacy theory as developed in *Griswold* to support a right to abortion was a huge stretch. As the Court itself stated, the Constitution itself "does not expressly mention any right of privacy." As Justice Black noted in his dissent in *Griswold*, various provisions of the Bill of Rights protect specific privacy interests, for example, the First Amendment's right of associational privacy, the Fourth Amendment's protection against unreasonable searches and seizures, and the Fifth Amendment's prohibition of compelled self-incrimination. But the Constitution does not create a general right of privacy. Recognition of a "general constitutional right to privacy" cannot be reconciled with the care with which the Framers of the Bill of Rights described the specific rights that were being secured.

Further, the concept of "privacy" is without firm form and all too apt to change (in Justice Black's words in *Griswold*, "broad, abstract and ambiguous"). *Roe*'s attempt to collect cases decided under the mantle of "privacy," a term that does not even appear in most of the cases cited, creates an artificial common denominator among a very disparate and largely unrelated group of cases that have nothing to do with the subject of abortion. This disconnect was freely admitted in the *Roe* decision:

> The situation [involving a pregnant woman and her unborn child] . . . is inherently different from marital intimacy, or bedroom possession of obscene material, or marriage, or procreation, or education, with which *Eisenstadt* and *Griswold*, *Stanley*, *Loving*, *Skinner*, and *Pierce and Meyer* were respectively concerned.

If a pregnant woman's decision whether or not to carry her

pregnancy to term is "inherently different" from all of the "privacy" cases on which the Court relied, then it is difficult to understand how those cases could support the recognition of a right to obtain an abortion.

Also worth noting is that most of the cases the *Roe* decision cited in support of its privacy theory were decided under one or another of the provisions in the Bill of Rights. *Roe* itself, however, derived the right of privacy (and a subsidiary right to abortion) from the liberty language in the due process clause of the Fourteenth Amendment, not from any of the specific guarantees in the Bill of Rights. That argument is contrary to the Court's express refusal in *Griswold* to rely upon the due process clause to derive a right of privacy.

Privacy argument diminished in later rulings

In *Planned Parenthood of Southeastern Pennsylvania v. Casey* (1992), the Court rejected the trimester framework in *Roe* while affirming its central holding that a woman has a right to abortion until fetal viability. The *Roe* decision defined "viable" as "potentially able to live outside the mother's womb, albeit with artificial aid." The justices in *Casey* acknowledged that viability might occur at twenty-three or twenty-four weeks, or sometimes even earlier in light of medical advances. The plurality made a subtle move away from the physician's-rights approach of *Roe* toward a patient's-rights approach by explicitly confirming that women had a constitutional right to abortion and further upholding the "essential holding" of *Roe*, stating that women have a right to choose abortion before viability and that this right cannot be unduly interfered with by the state. However, they asserted that this right is rooted in the due process clause of the Fourteenth Amendment, not in the privacy theory that underlay *Roe*.

Again, Justice Scalia most aptly summed up the decision in this excerpt from his dissent:

> Its length, and what might be called its epic tone, suggest that its authors believe they are bringing to an end a troublesome era in the history of our Nation and of our Court. . . . We should get out of this area, where we have no right to be, and where we do neither ourselves nor the country any good by remaining.

Scalia was widely notable for his directness in pointing out errors by other courts and judges. In a 2005 speech given at the (Woodrow) Wilson Center, he remarked:

> If you think aficionados of a living constitution want to bring you flexibility, think again. You think the death penalty is a good idea? Persuade your fellow citizens to adopt it. You want a right to abortion? Persuade your fellow citizens and enact it. That's flexibility.

Misuse of the Fourteenth Amendment

The Fourteenth Amendment provides that no State shall "deprive any person of life, liberty, or property, without due process of law." So due process is concerned with the process by which a person may be deprived of life, liberty, or property, not the substance of the law authorizing such deprivation. It is unlikely that the intent of the Framers of the Fourteenth Amendment was for the due process clause to serve as a bludgeon to demolish statutes the substance of which offends the sensibilities of a majority of justices who happen to be on the Supreme Court at a particular time.

Despite the internment of what may be called "economic" substantive due process (see the chapter on *Parrish*), "libertarian" substantive due process is alive and well. Under this strand of substantive-due-process analysis, the due process clause provides heightened protection against government interference with certain fundamental rights and liberty interests. *Roe v. Wade*, while replete with privacy theory, was ultimately based on the liberty language of the due process clause of the Fourteenth Amendment and, therefore, may justly be regarded as the modern paradigm of (libertarian) substantive due process analysis.

But *Roe* is at odds with the test the Court has been using for some decades to evaluate substantive due process claims. In determining whether an asserted liberty interest (or right) should be regarded as fundamental for purposes of substantive-due-process analysis (infringement of which would call for strict scrutiny review), the Supreme Court applies a dual test. First, there must be a "careful description" of the asserted fundamental liberty interest. Second, the interest, so described, must be firmly rooted in "the Nation's history, legal traditions, and practices."

An asserted interest in (or right to) abortion does not meet the second test. As much research has established, abortion was a crime in English and American common law, at least after "quickening" (that stage of pregnancy when the woman first detects fetal movement, usually at sixteen to eighteen weeks of gestation) and very possibly without such a limitation. With the gradual replacement of common-law crimes by statutory crimes in the nineteenth century, the overwhelming majority of states had made abortion at any stage of pregnancy a crime well before the Fourteenth Amendment was adopted in 1868. And the case law interpreting these statutes reveals that the principal, if not exclusive, purpose in enacting these statutes was to protect unborn human life, not (or not solely) to safeguard women from dangerous medical or surgical procedures. In light of these lookbacks, an interest in, or right to, abortion cannot be said to be firmly rooted in our history, legal traditions, and practices.

Unresolved issue

There is an unresolved area of abortion law: the scope of the health exception required by *Roe* and reaffirmed in *Casey*. The Court held that the states may prohibit abortion after viability "except when it is necessary to preserve the life or health of the mother." But the Court did not define the term "health." As things now stand, whether the open-ended "health" language of *Roe* is a limitation on the authority of the States to prohibit post-viability abortions remains an open question, but one that should be answered by a challenge to an appropriately drafted statute.

Conclusion

In recognizing a constitutional right to abortion, the Court in *Roe* undertook a legislative role, not a judicial one. It referenced the "profound problems of the present day," which included "the medical risks associated with pregnancy," a "distressful life and future" for the pregnant woman confronted with an unwanted pregnancy, "psychological harm," the difficulty in providing "child care," "the distress, for all concerned, associated with the unwanted child," and so forth.

The Court relied upon notions of "living constitutionalism," invoking the doctrine of substantive due process to create a right that is nowhere to be found in the text of the Constitution. This approach to adjudication is the prime mechanism of judges reading broad constitutional terms divorced from any textual or originalist moorings, thereby enabling their policy preferences. The due process clause was simply meant to protect the citizens from government abuse by ensuring that no one could be deprived of life, liberty, or property except by a fair process.

The fact that the Court has used the word "substantive" to describe a clause that is clearly about process creates an anachronism that defies language and logic. The Court here used the clause to support abortion rights without any reasoned justification after citing previous Supreme Court cases that erroneously established a broad constitutional right to privacy. The Court blithely asserted that this right "is broad enough to encompass a woman's decision whether or not to terminate her pregnancy."

The historical analysis used is also flawed. In an attempt to evaluate societal opinions about abortion throughout history, Blackmun looked to ancient societies, such as the Persian Empire, as well as the views of modern American lobbying organizations, but wholly ignored the state of abortion regulation at the time of the adoption of the Fourteenth Amendment. As Justice William Rehnquist said in his dissent, in 1868 "there were at least 36 laws enacted by state or territorial legislatures limiting abortion."

So, abortion liberty has no "roots" in the Nation's history, traditions, and legal practices. And the "national division" over the abortion controversy, which *Roe* created and *Casey* continued, will not end until the Supreme Court returns the issue of abortion to the states.

Moves for a constitutional amendment to outlaw abortion, especially all abortions, reveal a misunderstanding of the different purviews of the federal and state governments. Laws of everyday life and the family are enacted at the state level in our federal republic. This structure is useful because it places social and moral issues closer to the people and their values. And let's remember that before *Roe*, the abortion prohibition in most every state allowed for an exception in cases of rape, incest, and threats to the life of the mother. There will be no peace until this realm is returned to the state legislatures.

Consequences

Vast loss of lives

With the new ease of obtaining an abortion, the rate of pregnancy terminations increased dramatically after *Roe*. This Loxafamosity Ministries site has a tally (but it has not been updated since 2017):

W9-AA
https://abort73.com/abortion_facts/us_abortion_statistics/

Annual historical figures can be found at

W9-AB http://www.johnstonsarchive.net/policy/abortion/ab-unitedstates.html

Danger to the woman

In *Roe*, along with *Doe*, the right to abort for any reason was extended through the first six months of pregnancy. This "right" makes the United States almost as radical China, North

Korea, and Canada. Most nations limit abortion after about twenty weeks because of the health risks to women and the child. In the years since *Roe*, a plethora of medical evidence highlighting the harm to women from abortion, especially after the first trimester, has been amassed. For a survey of some of the complications in an article with full references to particular studies, visit Joel Ohman's AbortionFacts.com:

W9-AC http://www.abortionfacts.com/reardon/the-after-effects-of-abortion

Effect on attitude towards the value of life

The dismissal of a developing human being as just so much tissue is bound to affect a society's moral regard for the value of life. Since *Roe*, an activist judiciary, propelled by interest groups using the courts to remake the social order, has rendered opinions or laid the groundwork for an attack on the primacy of the family, an assault on the sanctity of life, and an abandonment of the rule of law. These activist judges have pushed their causes for infanticide, euthanasia, fetal experimentation, the abortifacient RU-486 drug, the "right to die," and physician-assisted suicide.

Growing acceptance of infanticide

Not only has this loss of respect for life had a profound impact on the euthanasia and health care debates, it also abets a thought pattern that if ending a human life is acceptable before birth, why isn't it acceptable after birth?

What is the difference between abortion and infanticide? In late 2018, several developments arose to proffer the idea that it might be OK to let die or indeed kill a child unexpectedly born during an abortion procedure. The early 2019 distressing comments of Virginia Governor Ralph Northum were well circulated:

> If a mother is in labor, I can tell you exactly what would happen. The infant would be delivered. The infant would be kept comfortable. The infant would be resuscitated if that's what the mother and the family desired, and then a discussion would ensue between the physicians and the mother.

Northam didn't say anything about "executing" infants, but he's effectively condoning allowing at least some infants to die after an unexpected birth during an abortion procedure.

Only from the life-is-cheap culture created by *Roe* would this discussion arise in a civilized society, the culture of which had long held without a second thought that life is sacred. This article by political science professor Justin Dyer in the publication of the Witherspoon Institute delineates how there is not much difference:

W9-AD https://www.thepublicdiscourse.com/2019/02/49302/

Increase in casual sex (?)

If an unwanted pregnancy from sex outside a marriage occurs, it's now easy for a man to say to himself before intimate contact and to the woman on her discovery of pregnancy, "Well, she/we can always just get an abortion." This observation is admittedly a conjecture, not something that research can prove.

Solutions

When the Court has spoken and its ruling has had the effect of law for a long time, the only solutions are a case where the Court overturns that decision or a successful constitutional amendment to return an issue to the states. So, the solution rests with the voters to do all they can to advance the campaigns of presidential candidates who will nominate only real constitutionalists for all federal judiciary vacancies. It is not a solution, as some abortion-opponent politicians have proposed, to advance federal legislation prohibiting abortion in some, much less, all cases. Such proposals just advertise the proposers' ignorance of federalism and the proper limits of jurisprudence in a federal republic.

In recent years some states have been passing abortion restrictions in the hope of getting a challenge before the Supreme Court and giving what appears to be a more conservative Court an opportunity to overturn *Roe*. Unfortunately, some of these proposed laws would prohibit all abortions; they are unlikely to sway the Court. The best of these bills contain the pre-*Roe* widely adopted exceptions for rape, incest, and the life of the mother. This February 2019 *New York Times* article describes some of these efforts:

W9-AE
https://www.nytimes.com/2019/02/08/us/abortion-laws.html

Footnote

In 1995, Norma McCorvey announced that she had quit her job at an abortion clinic and become an advocate of the Operation Rescue campaign to discourage women from seeking an abortion. She died in 2020.

In a 2022 case, *Dobbs v. Jackson Women's Health Organization, Roe* was overturned by a 5-4 vote. The ruling by Justice Samuel Alito argued that the Court making the taking of a life in an abortion a federal issue was at odds with the division of powers between the federal government and the states as outlined in the Constitution.

It should not have taken 49 years to correct this error, but considerable comfort can be had by observing that the Court can nullify an earlier mistake. Also of interest is Justice Thomas concurrence in which he suggested that the practice of substantial due process used in this case could well be reviewed in other cases that relied on a privacy interest not found the Constitution. Like perhaps *Lawrence v. Texas* and *Obergefell v. Hodges*?

For further reading

Won by Love by Norma McCorvey; 1998, Thomas Nelson

W9-AF https://www.barnesandnoble.com/w/won-by-love-norma-mccorvey/1115205169

Abuse of Discretion: The Inside Story of Roe v. Wade, by attorney Clarke D. Forsythe; 2013, Encounter Books

W9-AG https://www.encounterbooks.com/books/abuse-of-discretion-the-inside-story-of-roe-v-wade/

Life News is updated as needed, usually daily, with news on the pro-life front, including comments by politicians.

W9-AH http://www.lifenews.com

Stephanie Herman maintains a blog with some great articles on abortion and other issues of interest to women.

W9-AI http://www.rightgrrl.com/carolyn/infanticide.html

10~*Chevron U.S.A. v. Natural Resources Defense Council* (1984) and *Auer v. Robbins* (1997)

Society will develop a new kind of servitude which covers the surface of society with a network of complicated rules, through which the most original minds and the most energetic characters cannot penetrate. It does not tyrannize, but it compresses, enervates, extinguishes, and stupefies a people, till each nation is reduced to nothing better than a flock of timid and industrious animals, of which the government is the shepherd.
—Alexis de Tocqueville in *Democracy in America*

These cases are about administrative law and how, increasingly, federal government actions are less guided by acts of Congress than by decisions of federal departments and agencies, some of which act as both rule-maker and judge. The Woodrow Wilson progressive era marked the beginning of this government-knows-best trend. It was augmented substantially by the New Deal, which launched a vast bureaucracy and empowered it with broad governing authority. These powers are often exercised by independent agencies in a manner that is mostly independent of presidential control and substantially independent of political accountability.

The *Chenery* and *Seminole* precedents

A family fights the SEC

A 1943 case presaged the problems that autonomous agencies could present to constitutional law-making and law enforcement. The Securities and Exchange Commission (SEC) challenged a closely held firm, Federal Water Services Corporation, whose owners, members of the Chenery family (as C.T. Chenery Corporation) wished to reorganize in light of a 1935 law dealing with public utilities. They wanted to ensure that they would continue to own their firm. When the case ("Chenery I") got to the Supreme Court, the SEC lost because the Court found that neither a law nor an SEC-created regulation was being violated.

But the SEC kept the issue alive by bringing slightly different charges. In "Chenery II" (1947), the Court upheld the SEC's rejection of the reorganization plan on the basis that by this time, the SEC had formulated standards that prohibited the Cheneryss' plans and removed them from ownership.

No law passed by Congress was being violated, only a new agency regulation was, so we were on our way to being an administrative state, where the rule of law would have to take a back seat to the social expediency of "expert" administrators. Such a construct violates the basic idea of separation of powers, with discrete, non-overlapping powers for each branch and the answerability of all operatives in the administration of an elected executive.

Seminole Rock fights federal price controls

In 1945, the Court ruled in a way that gave wide latitude to agencies to interpret their own rules. The *Bowles v. Seminole Rock and Sand* ruling deferred to the Office of Price Administration (OPA), a World War II price control bureau, in a dispute over the price the rock company charged in a 1942 transaction. The company had a good case for charging a price at the time of an order that was higher than what the OPA later set before the date of delivery. One reaction to this decision was the 1946 Administrative Procedure Act (APA), which provided a framework for how federal agencies are to make and enforce regulations. It was, alas, perhaps not restraining enough, as we shall see in the *Chevron* and *Auer* cases.

The Chevron deference

The facts giving rise to *Chevron v. National Resources Defense Council* (1984) begin with the Clean Air Act Amendments of 1977, which imposed specific requirements on states that had not achieved the national air quality standards established by the Environmental Protection Agency (EPA) pursuant to earlier legislation.

One requirement was that such states establish a permit program regulating "new or modified major stationary sources" of air pollution. A permit could not be issued for such sources unless stringent conditions were met. The EPA promulgated regulations in 1981 to implement the permit requirement to allow a state to adopt a plant-wide definition of the term "stationary source." Under this regulation, an existing plant that contains several pollution-emitting devices may install or modify one piece of equipment without meeting the permit conditions if the alteration will not increase the total emissions from the plant. This understanding allowed a state to treat all pollution-emitting devices within the same industrial grouping as though they were encased within a single "bubble."

Enter the Natural Resources Defense Council

The Natural Resources Defense Council (NRDC) filed a petition for review in the Court of Appeals, which set aside the regulations embodying the "bubble concept" as contrary to law. NRDC then appealed to the Supreme Court.

Despite recognizing that the amended Clean Air Act does not explicitly define what Congress envisioned as a "stationary source" to which the permit program should apply and that the issue was not squarely addressed in the legislative history, the Supreme Court concluded that since the purpose of the non-attainment program was to improve, rather than merely maintain, air quality, a plant-wide definition was "inappropriate."

The Court deferred to the EPA's plant-wide definition as a permissible construction of the statutory term "stationary source," even though it admitted in its decision that the legislation and its history supported the conclusion by the Court of Appeals that Congress did not have a specific intention as to the applicability of the "bubble concept" in these cases.

Therefore, we now have "Chevron deference"—an agency's interpretation of an ambiguous statute must be permissible, which the court has defined to mean "rational" or "reasonable."

Auer et al v. Robbins: an agency's interpretation of its own ambiguous regulations

Thirteen years later, in *Auer et al. v. Robbins.*, the Court deferred to a Department of Labor agency regarding the interpretation of its own ambiguous rules and regulatory schemes, citing *Seminole Rock.*

In St. Louis, a group of police sergeants and a police lieutenant sued the Board of Police Commissioners, alleging that the Board failed to pay them overtime pay due to them under the Fair Labor Standards Act (FLSA). The Board argued that the policemen were not entitled to overtime pay because the officers fell under an exemption of the law for "any employee employed in a bona fide executive, administrative, or professional capacity" and were paid by salary rather than hours worked.

The officers relied on the fact that their pay could be docked for disciplinary reasons to show that they were not salarymen. However, there are few other ways to discipline government workers. The FLSA did not fully cover this particular employer–employee situation.

The salary-basis test was a creature of the Secretary of Labor's own regulations, not law. So, one could see how the Court would accede to Labor's interpretation of it. But such deference upsets the balance of power between the courts and federal agencies. The government cannot be faulted for arguing for deference, but judges should be faulted for accepting the government's argument. How is it fair in a court of justice for judges to defer to one of the litigants? In essence, the argument boils down to this —the government is populated by experts, and when they speak, we should accede. Such deference is found nowhere in the Constitution, the document that judges take an oath to support.

Chevron + *Auer*: deference is affirmed

Chevron and *Au*er together in effect give agencies broad scope to create regulations and rules and the authority to apply their interpretation where there is ambiguity in either the law passed by Congress or in the regulation promulgated by agencies themselves. These rulings have fueled the growth of the administrative state, a pervasive system of consolidated power that weakens the checks and balances carefully constructed by the Framers of the Constitution.

This deference conflicts with the 1946 Administrative Procedure Act, which Congress enacted to impose legal constraints on the administrative state. By these decisions and others, courts have interpreted the Act's requirements in a manner that is in tension with the text and original understanding of the law. The APA expressly ordered the courts to review *de novo* any and all administrative interpretations of the law. That directive is consistent with the long-standing common-law principle that courts must decide all legal issues independently.

Solutions

A revamp of the Administrative Procedures Act might be needed to more clearly require courts to abjure from deferring to agencies' interpretations.

Or the Court could reverse itself. Fortunately, the Court agreed in early 2019 to rule in a case that touches on both decisions. James Kisor, a Vietnam-veteran marine, was a participant in a 1965 search-and-destroy mission. In 1982, Kisor sought disability benefits from the Department of Veterans Affairs (VA) on the basis that he had developed post-traumatic stress disorder (PTSD) from his service.

The VA disagreed that he had PTSD and denied him disability benefits. Kisor appealed that decision in 2006, this time with additional documentation that was not available in 1982, including his service record. The VA granted benefits with this information, but with a start date of 2006 rather than 1982. That decision was based on the VA's interpretation of its own regulations that the new documents were not "relevant" to his 1982 request. The U.S. Court of Appeals for that circuit affirmed the VA's decision, referencing *Auer*; that is, it held that *Auer* gave the VA the authority to define the meaning of "relevant" in the regulation and put the burden on Kisor to demonstrate that the VA's ruling was not a valid interpretation. This *Reason Magazine* blog describes the issues:

W10-AA https://reason.com/volokh/2019/02/26/justice-department-asks-court-to-narrow

In June 2019, the Court ruled that the lower courts had to take another look at whether Kisor's combat records are "relevant" under the VA regulations. In so doing, the Court held that the lower courts may not reflexively defer to agency determinations of what their regulations mean.

Although the Court did not overrule *Auer* entirely, the ruling restricted when agency interpretations can bind the courts. All the tools of statutory construction must first be used by judges to determine whether a regulation is clear in the first place. An agency's interpretation of a regulation that is not clear must be within the range of ambiguity. The agency must also demonstrate its intent that the interpretation be controlling and that the agency is using its expertise in the particular subject matter. Judicial deference will no longer be given to ad hoc interpretations by low-level agency staff and after-the-fact litigation positions. Also, agency interpretations that inflict an "unfair surprise" on regulated parties will not receive deference by the courts.

These reforms are a move in the right direction, even though the result is that courts will still defer in limited circumstances. Many victims of agency authorities may now get a fairer hearing in their cases. Some courts might now heed the Court's limitations on *Auer* deference and subject agencies to meaningful checks and balances. But others may continue to "reflexively defer," as this ruling did not end judicial deference to agency regulatory interpretations entirely.

For further reading and action

The Upside-Down Constitution by Michael S. Greve; 2012, Harvard University Press

W10-AB http://www.hup.harvard.edu/catalog.php?isbn=9780674061910

Judicial Fortitude; The Last Chance to Rein in the Administrative State by Peter Wallison; 2018, Encounter Books

W10-AC
https://www.encounterbooks.com/books/judicial-fortitude/

Unmasking the Administrative State by John Marini; 2019, Encounter Books

W10-AD https://www.encounterbooks.com/books/unmasking-administrative-state/

Activist resource: Regulatory Transparency Project "Unlocking Innovation & Opportunity"
W10-AE https://regproject.org

11~*Bush v. Gore* (2000)

It is the mark of the mind untrained to take its own processes as valid for all men, and its own judgments for absolute truth.
–Aleister Crowley, *Magical and Philosophical Commentaries on The Book of the Law*

Reservations about Supreme Court decisions mostly take the form of a preference for a ruling other than the one made. Here the Court's error was in taking the case in the first place.

A tight election in the Sunshine State

The presidential election on November 3, 2000, was, in Florida, a horse race. George W. Bush, then governor of Texas, and Albert Gore, then vice president, were neck and neck. On November 8, the Florida Division of Elections reported that Bush won with 48.8% of the vote in Florida, a margin of victory of only 1,784 votes. (Pat Buchannan was also on the ballot.) This was the election of "hanging chads," "butterfly ballots," and questionable competence and motives of some county election officials.

The margin of victory being less than 0.5% of the votes cast, a statutorily mandated automatic machine recount began. On November 10th, with the machine recount finished in all but one county, Bush's margin of victory had decreased to 327 votes.

Florida's election laws allow a candidate to request that a

county do a manual recount; the Gore camp did just that—but only for four counties, all of which traditionally vote for Democrats. These counties granted the request and began manual recounts. However, Florida law required all counties to certify their election returns to the Florida Secretary of State within seven days of the election, and several of the counties reported that they probably would not be able to make this deadline.

On November 14, Secretary of State Katherine Harris issued a set of criteria by which she would determine whether to allow late filings. She also required any county seeking to make a late filing to submit to her by 2:00 p.m. the following day a written statement of the facts and circumstances justifying the late filing. Four counties submitted statements, and after reviewing the submissions Harris determined that none warranted an extension of the filing deadline. She further announced that after she received the certified returns of the overseas absentee ballots from each county, she would certify the results of the presidential election on Saturday, November 18.

The Florida Supreme Court intervenes

But, on November 17, the Florida Supreme Court (FSC) enjoined Harris from certifying the election while it heard appeals from the various cases in progress. On November 21, it allowed the manual recounts that had been started to continue and delayed certification until November 26.

On December 8, the FSC ordered a statewide manual recount, but the next day the U.S. Supreme Court voted 5–4 to stay the recount on the grounds that some of the votes were of questionable legality.

Bush appealed the earlier FSC decision to allow the manual

recount in only four counties as requested by the Gore camp. The U.S. Supreme Court said that the case could not be remanded to the Florida courts because Florida law required that the counting be completed by December 12 to meet the "safe harbor provision" created by federal law. The Bush argument was based on an equal-protection argument. That is, the recounts in only four Democrat-leaning counties with a suspect election process was not fair to him personally.

For a timeline of this story, see this 2008 article by *U.S. News & World Report*:

W11-AA https://www.usnews.com/news/articles/2008/01/17/the-legacy-of-hanging-chads

A more detailed account from the U.S. Election Atlas is at:

W11-AB https://uselectionatlas.org/INFORMATION/ARTICLES/pe2000timeline.php

The U.S. Supreme Court deems itself the rightful arbiter

What became *Bush v. Gore* attracted enormous public and media attention. There are procedures in the Constitution (12th Amendment) and federal law, especially the Electoral Count Act of 1887, to handle presidential election disputes within the two elected branches.

After the entire process took place in Florida, there might well have been competing claims as to which slate of electors should represent the state. The House of Representatives had full authority, and the responsibility, to decide this issue (Article II, Section 1). By granting certiorari in Bush's appeal, the Court diminished its standing and left the impression among many that it twisted the process to the political preference of its thin majority. And, as if confessing to its sloppy jurisprudence, the decision stated that the ruling was "to be limited to the present circumstances."

Out of several possible scenarios absent the Court's intervention, it is likely that Bush would have prevailed anyway. This outcome to the drama is discussed in this 2001 PBS story:

W11-AC https://www.pbs.org/newshour/nation/media-jan-june01-recount_04-03

Did this dispute properly belong in a federal court?

For several reasons, the Court should not have accepted this case for review: serious issues of standing and ripeness for review, the customary avoidance by federal courts of primarily political disputes, and the fact that taking the case amounted to a usurpation of state court jurisdiction.

Standing

Procedurally, *Bush v. Gore* came to the Supreme Court on a petition for a writ of certiorari brought by George W. Bush seeking review of the FSC's decision. After Florida Secretary of State Katherine Harris certified George W. Bush as the victor in Florida on Sunday, November 26, Gore filed a contest under Florida law. A Florida trial court judge in Leon County, Florida, held a hearing and ruled on December 4 in favor of Bush. The judge found that Gore needed to prove that it was probable that he would prevail if a recount were held and held that Gore had failed to do so.

The FSC immediately granted review, held a hearing on December 7, and on December 8 reversed the Florida trial court's decision to not conduct a recount. The FSC ruled that the trial court applied the wrong legal standard. Florida law states that a candidate can contest an election by demonstrating that enough illegal votes were cast to change the result. The FSC ruled that Gore met this burden, as there were many ballots that the machines did not count, making the result of this election uncertain. So, the FSC ordered the counting to begin immediately across the state. Per this order, counting started the next morning, Saturday, and the trial judge expected that the recount could be completed by 2:00 p.m. on the next day.

Questionable cert

Bush immediately sought U.S. Supreme Court review of the FSC's decision. On Saturday afternoon, December 9, the Supreme Court stayed the counting in Florida, granted review, and scheduled oral arguments for Monday, December 11. In other words, the case came to the U.S. Supreme Court on a petition for a writ of certiorari by the defendant in the lawsuit, George W. Bush. Bush's central claim was that counting of ballots without uniform standards violated equal protection.

But did Bush have standing to raise this claim? The Supreme Court long has said that the standing requirement is based on Article III limiting the federal courts to deciding "cases" and "controversies." Standing is thus jurisdictional, and courts must raise it on their own even if it is not challenged by one of the parties.

Where was the unequal treatment?

There was no reason to believe that the counting procedure would treat ballots for Bush any differently from ballots for Gore. Nor did Bush contend that he was treated unequally in the counting process. In other words, Bush was not claiming that he was being discriminated against in the counting of the uncounted votes. The equal protection issue was not discrimination between Bush and Gore, but rather discrimination among ballots. The only equal protection claim was that a voter's ballot might be disallowed and an identical ballot not counted. This claim made it irrelevant whether both ballots were for the same candidate or for different candidates; the argument was that to treat two similar ballots differently denied equal protection to the voter whose ballot was disallowed.

The U.S. Supreme Court has long maintained that Article III's limit on judicial power requires that a party show that he has personally suffered some actual or threatened injury. George W. Bush did not and could not claim that he was denied equal protection. The Florida Supreme Court did not discriminate against him in any way or treat him differently from candidate Gore. Bush did not have standing to raise an equal protection claim because he did not "personally suffer" any discrimination.

Where was the injury?

In earlier cases, the Supreme Court had expressly applied standing in election matters, such as *United States v. Hays* (1995), where the Court held that only a person residing within an election district may argue that the lines for the district were unconstitutionally drawn in violation of equal protection. Bush did not have standing in *Bush v. Gore*. Bush's injury of not winning the presidency was distinct from the injury to the voters in having their ballots counted unequally. Because Bush did not vote in Florida, he could not assert this injury, under *Hays*. Further, the Supreme Court long has said that the absence of a plaintiff with standing indicates that the matter is to be left to the political process and not to the courts.

The Supreme Court has said that standing is founded on concern about the proper and properly limited role of the courts in a democratic society. In *Bush v. Gore*, the Court should have explained why it afforded Bush standing to raise the claims of Florida voters.

Ripeness

In addition to standing, there was a question of whether this case was ripe for review. The ripeness doctrine serves to exclude from federal court matters that are premature for review because the injury is speculative and may never occur. This doctrine is based on Article III's limiting federal court action to cases and controversies. So even if Bush had standing to raise the claims of Florida voters, there was an issue as to whether this claim was ripe for review.

The issues before the Supreme Court were not ripe for review for several reasons. Would the counting of votes deny equal protection? A constitutional violation would arise only if similar ballots were treated differently in the counting process, but it could not be known if this would happen until all votes were counted and the trial judge in Florida ruled on all of the challenges. So, it was purely speculative whether there would be a problem with similar ballots being treated differently.

The Court was focusing on inequalities that already had occurred. The opinion pointed to differences in counting between Miami–Dade and Palm Beach counties. However, the counting that already had been done was not the issue before the Supreme Court, which was whether the counting should continue.

Experience was not predictive of what was to occur because of a critical change: a single judge was overseeing the recount under the FSC's decision. He was to hear all of the disputes and potentially could eliminate any inequalities by applying a uniform standard.

Justice Stevens emphasized exactly this point in his dissent. He wrote:

> Admittedly, the use of differing substandards for determining voter intent in different counties employing similar voting systems may raise serious concerns. Those concerns are alleviated—if not eliminated—by the fact that a single impartial magistrate will ultimately adjudicate all objections arising from the recount process.

But Stevens did not draw a key conclusion from his observation: that the challenge to the counting was not ripe for review. Only after the recount was completed could the parties claim that there was inequality and thus a constitutional violation.

In other words, the Supreme Court improperly treated an "as applied" equal-protection challenge as if Bush were arguing that the Florida election law was unconstitutional on its face. He was not. His argument was that counting without uniform standards denied equal protection. But again, this is an equal-protection violation only if, after the counting and the resolution of disputes by the judge, similar ballots are treated differently, and whether that occurred could not be known in advance.

Bush v. Gore was not ripe for an even more basic reason: George W. Bush might well have ended up ahead after the counting. In that event, there obviously would have been no need for the Supreme Court to decide his appeal. Its taking this case conflicts with the history of the Supreme Court repeatedly holding that a case is not ripe when it is unknown whether an injury will be suffered.

So, the case was not ripe for review on December 9, when the stay was issued, or December 11, when the case was heard, or December 12, when it was decided. It would have been ripe only after all the counting was done if (a) Gore came out ahead in Florida and (b) Bush could present evidence of inequalities in how the ballots were counted. Until and unless these eventualities occurred, the case was not ripe and should have been dismissed.

The Political-Question Doctrine

The Supreme Court has held that certain allegations of unconstitutional government conduct should not be ruled on by federal courts, even though all jurisdictional and other justiciability requirements are met. The Court has said that constitutional interpretation in these areas should be left to the politically accountable branches of government: the President and Congress. In other words, the term "political-question doctrine" refers to subject matter that the Court deems inappropriate for judicial review. Although there is an allegation that the Constitution has been violated, the federal courts refuse to rule and instead dismiss the case, leaving the constitutional question to be resolved through the political process.

Some factors that have persuaded the Court not to rule in political cases have included the strangeness of the issue that suggests its intractability to a principled resolution; the possibility that its momentousness might lead to an unbalanced judicial judgment; the concern that judicial judgment should be ignored but will not be; and the self-doubt of an institution that is electorally unaccountable.

Very much a political case

These reservations were particularly appropriate in this case. Never before in history had the Supreme Court decided a presidential election. The Court ruled that counting the ballots without uniform standards would be unequal, but no decision had ever found that variations among counties in election practices were unconstitutional. Nor did the Court explain why this inequality was impermissible, while many other disparities in Florida, such as differences in ballots and voting machines, were constitutional.

Indeed, the Court seemed aware of the problems with applying equal protection to such variances among counties and with opening the door to challenges to virtually every election because of reliance on local election officials. As noted above, the opinion said that the ruling was "limited to the present circumstances" and that "the problem of equal protection in election processes generally presents many complexities." This admission certainly reminds one of the reservations the Court had previously applied to political cases. And would not engaging with this case invite an unbalanced judicial judgment?

Bush v. Gore cost the Supreme Court enormously in terms of its credibility. Over forty-nine million people voted for Gore, and probably all of them regarded the Court's decision as a partisan ruling by a Republican majority. And surely many Republicans must have been embarrassed that it appeared that their man won by special dispensation from an outside force rather than in the normal electoral marketplace.

State adjudication of its laws usurped by SCOTUS

The Supreme Court's opinion held that counting the uncounted votes without standards violates equal protection and that a Florida law prevented the counting from continuing past December 12.

Assuming that there were inequalities in the counting that violated the Constitution, there were two remedies: count none of the uncounted ballots or count all of the ballots with uniform standards. The latter would involve remanding the case to the FSC for the development of standards and such relief as that court deemed appropriate.

This dispute was one that the Florida laws and courts could have and should have handled, as there was no state law that required that the counting had to be completed by November 12. The sole authority for the Supreme Court's conclusion was one statement by the FSC.

That statement was made in a very different context and when the FSC was not faced with the issue posed by the Supreme Court's ruling. After the Supreme Court decided on December 12 that counting without standards violated equal protection, the issue became what remedy was appropriate under Florida law: continue the counting past December 12 or end the recount to meet the December 12 deadline.

The Supreme Court could not possibly know how the FSC would resolve this issue because it had never occurred before. Florida decisions emphasized the importance of making sure that every vote is accurately counted. The FSC might have relied on this preference to continue the counting past December

12. Alternatively, the court might have ended the counting, treating December 12 as a firm deadline in Florida. *The vote-counting dispute was a question of Florida law to be decided by the Florida Supreme Court.*

Conclusion

Notwithstanding the "limited to the present circumstances" qualification, *Bush v. Gore* was a massive unconstitutional usurpation of powers that belonged to elected state and federal zones. It is ironic that the five justices in the majority were those who most professed a need for judicial restraint, championed the rightful powers of the states, and promoted restrictive justiciability doctrines. In this case, those five justices abandoned all of these principles and surely provided subtle fodder to influence future justices to enlarge the scope of cases they would vote to consider and judgments they could make.

Justice Stevens netted out the damage well in this excerpt from his dissent:

> [The] position [of] the majority of this Court can only lend credence to the most cynical appraisal of the work of judges throughout the land. It is confidence in the men and women who administer the judicial system that is the true backbone of the rule of law. Time will one day heal the wound to that confidence that will be inflicted by today's decision. One thing, however, is certain. Although we may never know with complete certainty the identity of the winner of this year's Presidential *election*, the identity of the loser is perfectly clear. It is the Nation's confidence in the judge as an impartial guardian of the rule of law.

So, in *Bush v. Gore* we had an unnecessary intrusion by the Court in a matter that had a regular mechanism for resolution and which intrusion diminished the prestige of the Court and might have created a precedent for unwarranted interference in future election disputes.

For further reading

Judging the Supreme Court: Constructions of Motives in Bush v. Gore (Rhetoric & Public Affairs) 1st Edition
by Clarke Rountree; Michigan State University, 2007

Bush v. Gore: Exposing the Hidden Crisis in American Democracy: Abridged and Updated (Landmark Law Cases and American Society) by Charles L. Zelden; University Press of Kansas, 2010

12~*Lawrence v. Texas* (2003) and *Obergefell v. Hodges* (2015)

How dreadful it is when the right judge judges wrong!
—Sophocles, *Antigone*

Most observers of history and government would agree to describe the United States of America as a federal constitutional republic: a republic because laws are made by elected representatives, constitutional because it has a written fundamental law and organizing structure, and federal because it has states that have powers to tax and make and enforce laws within their borders.

One basic idea of federalism is that states legislate or administer common law over the broad scope of everyday life to enable an orderly and productive society and ensure that its laws do not conflict with the U.S. Constitution. Thus, laws on a host of issues differ from state to state as their citizens direct their elected legislators, while matters that are the purview of the federal government's constitutional areas of activity are addressed with laws passed by Congress. These laws apply across the nation and its territories, and where there is a conflict, federal law prevails.

As state legislators are elected by the citizens of the state, such laws naturally reflect the values of the majority, whether they are derived from religious convictions or personal philosophy about what public policies make for a well-ordered society. The most obvious are laws against murder, theft, and assault. The will of the majority is not absolute—the Constitution recognizes that the people have certain rights that the majority may not override, and in protecting these rights, the courts must rule according to the law and the Constitution, not the personal opinions of judges.

One area of state legislation is personal behavior that a state deems dangerous or immoral and that, when practiced, may diminish society or may cause some other unfavorable consequence to the parties directly involved, to others, or to society as a whole. So, the states have laws about families, marriage, children, sexual behavior, and abortion; they generally comport with natural law and common sense when not distorted or invalidated by unelected tribunals.

It is in these areas that the most damage by courts at all levels has been done in recent years. The damage is both in the resulting bad public policy and also, even worse, to the process of representative government.

Powers of the states commandeered by the Court

For its long-term societal damage, the most destructive Supreme Court ruling in the modern era could well be *Lawrence v. Texas* (June 2003). In this 6–3 ruling, the Court struck down Texas's sodomy law and, by extension, sodomy laws in thirteen other states, making adult same-sex sexual activity legal in every U.S. state and territory.

Lawrence held that the Court had viewed the liberty interest too narrowly in a 1986 case and that intimate consensual sexual conduct was part of the liberty protected by substantive due process under the Fourteenth Amendment.

Laws on sex and views on privacy

As of 1960, every state had an anti-sodomy law. This fact tells us something about what most citizens thought about same-sex activity. In challenges to these laws, most judges were mostly unsympathetic to the substantive due process claims raised: that such acts are, by previous court decisions, beyond the reach of governmental interference.

Enter *Griswold*

As we saw in Chapter 9, *Griswold v. Connecticut* (1965) struck down the state's Comstock Act of 1873, which barred the use of contraceptives by married couples. To be sure, this was a nutty law, and by the 1950s only Massachusetts had a similar one. There was nothing to prevent the voters of both states making clear to their legislatures that this law should be nixed. But did it conflict with rights found in the Constitution?

For the first time, the Supreme Court recognized, at least for married couples, a right to privacy, drawing on the Fourth Amendment's protection of private homes from searches and seizures without a warrant based on probable cause, the Fifth Amendment's guarantee of due process of law, and the Ninth Amendment's assurance that rights not specified in the Constitution are "retained by the people."

Penumbras and emanations

Although the law in question was unwise, the reasoning in the 7–2 ruling was a strange example of overreaching to come up with a justification for overturning it. The decision's author, Justice Douglas, described the right of marital privacy to be found in the "penumbras" and "emanations" of other constitutional protections, such as the self-incrimination clause of the Fifth Amendment and the freedom of association clause of the First Amendment.

The ruling is key, as it was the opening wedge in a series of decisions that chipped away at state laws regarding moral restraints on sexual activity. In 1972, *Eisenstadt v. Baird* expanded the scope of sexual privacy rights to unmarried persons. And in 1973, the choice to have an abortion was found by seven justices to be protected by the Constitution in *Roe v. Wade*.

In *Bowers v. Hardwick* (1986), the Supreme Court heard a constitutional challenge to sodomy laws brought by a man who had been arrested—but was not prosecuted—for engaging in oral sex with another man in his home. The Court rejected this challenge in a 5–4 decision. Justice Byron White's majority opinion emphasized that *Eisenstadt* and *Roe* had recognized only a right to engage in procreative sexual activity and that long-standing moral antipathy toward homosexual sodomy was enough to argue against the notion of a right to sodomy.

By the time of the *Lawrence* decision, nine states (Alabama, Florida, Idaho, Louisiana, Mississippi, North Carolina, South Carolina, Utah, and Virginia) still banned consensual sodomy without respect to the sex of those involved, and four (Texas, Kansas, Oklahoma, and Missouri) prohibited same-sex couples from engaging in sodomy.

The argument

The origin of *Lawrence v. Texas* is unusual in that the circumstances of the arrest may have been contrived by the men arrested to bring their agenda to the courts. That is the argument documented in Robert Riley's book *Making Gay OK: How*

Rationalizing Homosexual Behavior Is Changing Everything. Just as the duo planned, the legal proceedings found their way to the Supreme Court.

Justice Anthony Kennedy wrote the majority opinion, which Justices John Paul Stevens, David Souter, Ruth Bader Ginsburg, and Stephen Breyer joined. He wrote, "The petitioners [John Lawrence and Tyrone Garner] are entitled to respect for their private lives. The State cannot demean their existence or control their destiny by making their private sexual conduct a crime." Kennedy reviewed the assumption the court made in *Bowers*, using the words of Chief Justice Burger's concurring opinion in that case: that "[condemnation of [homosexual practices] is firmly rooted in Judeo-Christian moral and ethical standards."

Kennedy reviewed the history of legislation that criminalized certain sexual practices without regard for the sex of those involved. He cited the Model Penal Code of 1955 (which relied on Kinsey's fraudulent sex research), the Wolfenden Report of 1963, and a 1981 decision of the European Court of Human Rights.

He endorsed the views Justice Stevens had outlined in his dissent in *Bowers* and wrote: "*Bowers* was not correct when it was decided, and it is not correct today. It ought not to remain binding precedent. *Bowers v. Hardwick* should be and now is overruled." The majority decision also held that the intimate, adult consensual conduct at issue was part of the liberty protected by the substantive component of Fourteenth Amendment due process protection. Holding that "the Texas statute furthers no legitimate state interest which can justify its intrusion into the personal and private life of the individual," the Court struck down the anti-sodomy law as unconstitutional.

The issues of whether there is a "legitimate state interest" in a law and whether a law is "rational" are troubling. Neither a state's constitution nor the U.S. Constitution gives a court the power to judge a law on that basis; only legislative bodies can do so. The decision also ignored the issue of federalism, which respects the powers of the states to make laws that reflect the values of their citizens and do not conflict with the Constitution.

Contrary arguments

While the public awaited the Court's decision, there was much discussion of the case. Senator Rick Santorum in April 2003 referred to the arguments in *Lawrence* when asked his views on homosexuality:

> We have laws in states, like the one at the Supreme Court right now, that has sodomy laws and they were there for a purpose. . . And if the Supreme Court says that you have the right to consensual sex within your home, then you have the right to bigamy, you have the right to polygamy, you have the right to incest, you have the right to adultery. You have the right to anything. . . . It all comes from, I would argue, this right to privacy that doesn't exist in my opinion in the United States Constitution, this right that was created . . . in *Griswold*.

The decision

The decision said otherwise: the six-justice majority declared that a state could not criminalize homosexual sodomy based on an expansive interpretation of the nonexistent privacy provisions in the Constitution. Justice Antonin Scalia wrote a dissent, joined by Chief Justice Rehnquist and Justice Thomas. Scalia objected to the Court's decision to revisit *Bowers*, pointing out many decisions from lower courts that relied on it that might need to be reconsidered. He noted that the same rationale used to overturn *Bowers* could have been used to reverse *Roe v. Wade*, which the justices in the majority in *Lawrence* had recently (in 1992) upheld in *Planned Parenthood v. Casey*. Scalia also criticized the majority opinion for failing to give the same respect to *stare decisis* (previous rulings) that three of those in the majority had insisted on in *Casey*.

The prescient Scalia wrote that if the court was not prepared to validate laws based on moral choices as it had done in *Bowers*, state laws against bigamy, same-sex marriage, adult incest, prostitution, adultery, fornication, bestiality, and obscenity could be called into question by this decision:

> If moral disapprobation of homosexual conduct is "no legitimate state interest" for purposes of proscribing that conduct . . . what justification could there possibly be for denying the benefits of marriage to homosexual couples exercising the liberty protected by the Constitution?"

He further wrote:

> Today's opinion is the product of a Court, which is the product of a law-profession culture that has largely signed on to the so-called homosexual agenda, by which I mean the agenda promoted by some homosexual activists directed at eliminating the moral opprobrium that has traditionally

> attached to homosexual conduct . . . . The Court has taken sides in the culture war, departing from its role of assuring, as a neutral observer, that the democratic rules of engagement are observed.

Justice Scalia cited the majority's concern that the criminalization of sodomy could be the basis for discrimination against homosexuals as evidence that the majority ignored the views of most Americans:

> So imbued is the Court with the law profession's anti-anti-homosexual culture, that it is seemingly unaware that the attitudes of that culture are not obviously "mainstream;" that in most States what the Court calls "discrimination" against those who engage in homosexual acts is perfectly legal. Let me be clear that I have nothing against homosexuals, or any other group, promoting their agenda through normal democratic means . . . The majority's invention of a brand-new "constitutional right" showed it was impatient of democratic change.

Of concern in this decision is the possible influence of foreign law on the majority. Among the amicus briefs submitted on the plaintiff side was one by six law professors who specialize in foreign and comparative constitutional law and human rights. They argued that the Court should consider that many democracies have legalized same-sex marriage and been able to successfully balance the rights of religious institutions with the rights of individuals to marry. They also contended that the Court should recognize the impact its decision may have on the rest of the world. The threat of American judges and justices referring to foreign law in their reasoning has been increasing ever since a decision 1981 by the European Court of Human Rights.

Consequences

The most immediate consequence of this judicial power grab was in hyper-liberal Massachusetts. In November of that year (2003), the Supreme Judicial Court, following the thread of *Lawrence*, decided (4–3) in *Goodrich v. Department of Public Health* that marriage was a protected right in the Massachusetts Constitution regardless of what combination of sexes it might entail. The ruling, written by South African–born Margaret Marshall, gave the General Court (the Massachusetts state legislature) six months to legalize same-sex marriage.

The assault on federalism and republican process

Leaving aside for the moment the Court's assault on traditional values, the very act of a court ordering the legislature to make a law is totally out of bounds. In a republic, legislation is the duty and power of an elected legislature whose members are dependent on voters for their reelection. If a republic is a government ruled by law and its laws are made by representatives elected by the citizens, then after May 16, 2004, citizens of Massachusetts could no longer say that the Commonwealth of Massachusetts is a republic. John Adams, author of the Massachusetts Constitution (the oldest still operating government charter in the world) would not be happy to learn of this assault on the separation of powers. It is indeed strange that the Court would find a right to same-sex marriage in a document written by the very conservative and dour John Adams!

Did not most of our founding generation launch a revolution to ensure representative government? The General Court made no such change to the marriage law. The lack of a new law would have been the end of this grab for power by the judiciary, but for the actions of Governor Willard Mitt Romney. Whether from not reading carefully the November 2003 decision or out of concern about not losing even a small voting bloc, Romney decided on his own to implement homosexual marriage. Romney could have led in this area by pointing out how out-of-bounds the Supreme Judicial Court was. But no, Romney buckled completely and gave Marshall and her three partners everything they wanted by administratively ordering a revision of the state marriage license from "bride" and "groom" to "Party A" and "Party B." He also ordered that any town or city clerk was to be fired if he or she refused to issue a license to a same-sex couple.

So today we have a combination of the two branches of government that don't make laws having made one anyway, the people be damned. To add insult to injury, the General Court in July 2007 refused to permit the voters to vote on a constitutional amendment referendum supported by 170,000+ voters to define marriage in Massachusetts in its traditional form.

Resistance emerges

One brave group, Waltham, Massachusetts–based MassResistance, came forward to oppose the court action. This pro-family-values organization was founded in 1995 as the Parents' Rights Coalition to counter pro-homosexual propaganda and radical sex education in Boston-area public schools. The group also vigorously defends traditional marriage and representative government. In early 2004, they launched an effort to remove the four Massachusetts justices. Their argument was based on Article 8 of the Massachusetts Constitution, which permits the legislature, with the concurrence of the Governor's Council, to remove an errant justice for cause without a formal impeachment proceeding or consent of the governor. This provision was written in by John Adams, who knew how arrogant appointed judges could become.

Given the overwhelmingly liberal tilt of the Massachusetts legislature, it was no surprise that this effort was not successful. But the organization has been very active conveying the societal consequences of same-sex marriage to other states and countries under similar threat. Their booklet *What Same-Sex "Marriage" Has Done to Massachusetts* by MassResistance director Brian Camenker is available online in book form at:

W12-AA http://www.massresistance.org/docs/marriage/effects_of_ssm_2012/index.html

and in a video at:

W12-AB https://www.youtube.com/watch?v=2ZXzUpzHLkA.

But the real consequences of the Massachusetts mess would eventually affect other parts of the country in the march toward state-sanctioned sodomy. Several states passed laws or amendments to clarify and reinforce traditional marriage. But in other states (especially in the northeast), other actors—such as city clerks, lower-court judges, and state supreme court judges—took it upon themselves to decide against prevailing law or practice. Connecticut passed a same-sex civil union law in 2005, but no state legislature passed a same-sex marriage law until Vermont did so in April 2009. Maine fell in the same way in May 2009 (the law was repealed by referendum in

November only to return via another statewide vote in 2012). Then New Hampshire, a month later. New York went over to the dark side in June 2011. Other states to pass and enact such legislation: Washington in February 2012; Maryland in March 2012; Rhode Island in May 2013; Delaware and Minnesota in May 2013; and Hawaii and Illinois in November 2013.

However out of touch with common sense and traditional values they are, at least these states changed marriage policy through a process appropriate to a federal republic. More destructive were the cases where marriage policy was changed by judicial fiat, sometimes at the local level, sometimes at the state level. Statewide diktats from their highest court were issued in New Jersey in 2006, California and Connecticut in 2008, and Iowa in 2009.

Further consequences: state voter initiative scuttled and law of Congress overturned

California: voters' preference ignored by district court

Though family law has been a state matter in these United States, the U.S. Supreme Court in June 2013 waded in again anyway in two disturbing assaults on representative government and state powers. The most destructive was *Hollingsworth v. Perry*, in which it dismissed a suit brought by sponsors of Proposition 8 ("Prop 8"), an initiative to affirm in the California Constitution that marriage is only between a man and a woman. Prop 8 won by 52% in November 2008; it was a response to a ruling by the California Supreme Court in May of that year that state statutes prohibiting same sex marriage violate the state constitution. That is, the U.S. Supreme Court majority said that the lower courts were without jurisdiction to consider the appeal of the proposition sponsors because a private party could not replace a state legal office if the latter refused to appeal.

Two same-sex couples filed a lawsuit, *Perry v. Schwarzenegger* (later *Hollingsworth v. Perry*), against the initiative in the United States District Court for the Northern District of California. In August 2010, Chief Judge Vaughan Walker ruled that the amendment was unconstitutional under both the due process and equal protection clauses of the Fourteenth Amendment since it purported to remove rights only from a disfavored class, with no rational basis. The official proponents' justifications for the measure were analyzed in over fifty pages covering eighty findings of fact. The state government supported the ruling and refused to defend the amendment. The decision was stayed pending appeal by the proponents of the initiative.

The reasoning of Judge Walker was obviously based on what he thought public policy should be and evidenced a hostility toward natural law typical of rulings against traditional marriage in similar decisions. His sexual orientation might have been a contributing factor to his policy preference, but in any event it did not seem to occur to him that his job was not to set public policy but to rule on whether the proposition was correctly initiated and submitted to the voters. It had already passed muster in state courts as eligible for the ballot.

The Supremes punt

On June 26, 2013, the Supreme Court issued its decision in *Hollingsworth v. Perry*, ruling that proponents of initiatives such as Proposition 8 did not possess legal standing in their own right to defend the resulting law in federal court, either before the Supreme Court or (previously) before the Ninth Circuit Court of Appeals. Therefore, the Supreme Court both dismissed the appeal and directed the Ninth Circuit to vacate (withdraw) its decision, which had upheld the district court ruling. The decision left Walker's 2010 judgment intact. Two days later, the Ninth Circuit lifted its stay of the district court's ruling, enabling Governor Jerry Brown to order same-sex marriage officiating to resume.

One could never be sure what Justice Kennedy would do, but he got it right in his dissent in *Hollingsworth* (joined by Justices Alito, Thomas, and Sotomayor). He noted that voter initiatives exist precisely for those times when voters believe the state was insufficiently responsive to their concerns—as a way for the people to assert their rights. He was concerned that the ruling would give elected officials the ability to nullify such voter-initiated laws by merely choosing not to defend them. Kennedy wrote:

> In the end, what the Court fails to grasp or accept is the basic premise of the initiative process. And it is this. The essence of democracy is that the right to make law rests in the people and flows to the government, not the other way around. Freedom resides first in the people without need of a grant from government.

He further wrote that the majority opinion:

> has implications for the twenty-six states that use an initiative or popular referendum system. The court's reasoning does not take into account the fundamental principles or the practical dynamics of the initiative system in California, which uses this mechanism to control and to bypass public

> officials—the same officials who would not defend the initiative, an injury the Court now leaves unremedied.

Federal law regarding marriage overturned

But Justice Kennedy (and four other "liberal" justices) got it wrong in a separate ruling that day in 2013. In *Windsor v. United States*, the majority forgot that Congress, representing the people, has the power to decide how public funds are spent at the federal level. Mainly as a response to a 1990 suit in Hawaii by three same-sex couples who argued that the state's prohibition of same-sex marriage violated Hawaii's constitution, Congress passed the Defense of Marriage Act ("DOMA") in 1996. This law prohibited giving federal benefits to same-sex couples. The Act had nothing to say about what states did with their money or their laws on marriage, but the Court, in *Windsor*, thought it knew better than Congress and President Clinton, who had signed it, and nixed DOMA.

Starting in late 2013, taking a cue from the *Windsor* ruling, proponents of same-sex marriage brought a series of suits that worked their way up to state superior courts or federal district courts. Judges took it upon themselves to overturn state marriage policies based on the notion that prohibiting same-sex marriage violated equal protection clauses in the federal or state constitutions. That thinking would render any law unconstitutional if it recognized differences between the sexes by affording women a bit more protection in family law. Among the states affected were Utah in late 2013 and Oregon, Pennsylvania, Indiana, Kentucky, Colorado, Florida, Virginia, and Wisconsin in 2014. But in this same period, a federal district judge upheld Louisiana's ban on same-sex marriage. A mess ensues when courts legislate!

The Supreme Court should have supported government by, of, and for the people by overturning Judge Walker and letting the winning vote in the Prop 8 initiative stand. And it should have respected the power of Congress to make decisions on federal benefits and expenditures. By its reasoning in these decisions, especially regarding DOMA, the Court laid the groundwork for overturning all state laws that define marriage as between a man and a woman instead of restoring the power of the people to control their government at all levels.

More confusion: federal district courts assume legislative powers

With such confusion, thirty-two states that either allow same-sex marriage or have banned it asked the U.S. Supreme Court in September 2014 to settle the issue once and for all. Fifteen states that allow gay marriage, led by Massachusetts, filed a brief asking the justices to take up three cases from Virginia, Utah, and Oklahoma and overturn bans. And seventeen other states, led by Colorado, that have banned the practice asked the Court to hear cases from Utah and Oklahoma to clear up a "morass" of lawsuits but didn't urge the Court to rule one way or another.

The states that wished to maintain traditional marriage made a big mistake by asking a court to resolve the confusion that was started by courts! Instead, they should have, in unison, given notice that they would defy the courts if their marriage laws were overturned, as such decisions are not within the courts' power in a federal republic.

The U.S. Supreme Court declined in October 2014 to hear

appeals from five states of federal appellate court rulings striking down state marriage laws. The decision not to take these cases meant that Virginia, Wisconsin, and Utah had to begin recognizing marriages of persons of the same sex. Since the federal appeals courts for those states cover other states, six more states would have been forced to recognize same-sex marriages, even if the voters or elected bodies of those states chose to define civil marriage as only the union of one man and one woman.

Ryan Anderson, William E. Simon Fellow at The Heritage Foundation, a conservative think tank, criticized the Court's decision because it left in place poor court decisions that trampled upon democratic processes, or government by the governed:

> This is an unfortunate setback for sound constitutional self-government and a setback for a healthy marriage culture. Same-sex marriage supporters and traditional marriage supporters both have reasonable arguments, . . . so the decision on how to define marriage for the purposes of state law should be made through democratic processes, not forced upon states by judges. In a system of limited constitutional self-government, the people and their elected representatives should be making decisions about marriage policy. And there are reasonable arguments on both sides of this debate. Judges should not insert their own policy preferences about marriage and declare them to be required by the Constitution.

Tony Perkins of the Family Research Council also warned that the decision undermines democracy and the rule of law:

> Even more alarming, lower court judges are undermining our form of government and the rights and freedoms of citizens to govern themselves. This judicially led effort to force same-sex "marriage" on people will have negative consequences for our Republic, not only as it relates to natural marriage but also undermining the rule of and respect for law.

More confusion at the district level

In February 2014, a judge in the U.S. Fifth District Court of Appeals struck down the Texas ban on same-sex marriage but stayed the decision so it did not go into effect. But in November, a divided federal appeals court in Cincinnati upheld prohibitions against same-sex marriage in four states. In January 2015, the Supreme Court announced that it would consider these cases, which it did in hearings in April. But all of these cases became moot after the *Obergefell* decision.

Other consequences, perhaps intended

Harassment of independent business proprietors

After laws or judicial rulings permitted same-sex marriage, many state and local jurisdictions began to enact legislation to prohibit discrimination against same-sex couples by businesses. Many tales have unfolded of bakers, florists, and videographers with moral objections to same-sex unions being forced either to close down or violate their beliefs by participating creatively in events that they find morally objectionable.

For example, in 2012, a suburban Denver baker, Jack Phillips, was sued by a male–male couple after he refused to make a cake to celebrate their marriage. The baker said he is deeply religious and that making the cake would violate the Christian principles by which he runs his Lakewood bakery. An administrative law judge ruled against Phillips; the commission upheld that decision, finding that Phillips's refusal violated the state's public accommodation law that requires businesses to serve customers regardless of their sexual orientation. So, he reluctantly stopped making wedding cakes. Are we still living in a free country?

W12-AC http://denver.cbslocal.com/2014/05/30/bakery-will-stop-making-wedding-cakes-after-losing-discrimination-case/

In June 2018, the Supreme Court found (7–2) that the Commission's first action against Phillips was infected with anti-religious animus. But Phillips continued to be harassed by LGBT activists. He and the Commission reached a truce in March 2019.

W12-AD https://dailycaller.com/2019/03/05/jack-phillips-masterpiece-colorado/

Alas, the Phillips decision did not clear the air. In 2013, a florist in Washington state, Baronelle Stutzman, declined to provide flowers for a wedding of two females on religious and moral grounds. The couple sued her and her business under a Washington anti-discrimination law. The case got to the U.S. Supreme Court in 2018 but was not argued by the time of the *Phillips* decision. So, the Court returned the case to Washington for reconsideration given its finding for Mr. Phillips. But in June 2019, the Washington Supreme Court again ruled against Stutzman. State coercion one, freedom zero. Her cases against the state and the ACLU are still ongoing as of publication. The Alliance Defending Freedom is assisting with both cases.

W12-AE https://www.wnd.com/2019/06/court-rules-against-florist-who-refused-same-sex-couple/

Hints of new forms of marriage

But wait —there's more confusion in store: social conservatives who have argued for marriage solely between one man and one woman have long warned that allowing same-sex marriage would ultimately lead to allowing polygamy, or who knows what combinations, if the only basis of marriage is that the persons involved love each other.

In December 2013, U.S. District Court Judge Clark Waddoups declared that Utah laws criminalizing polygamy are unconstitutional. More specifically, he ruled that laws against cohabitation of unmarried persons are no longer legal. The judge's ruling did not say that Utah must recognize multiple marriages, but the crack in the door may have been opened for all sorts of collections to become a married unit.

As Tony Perkins of the Family Research Council put it:

> Same-sex marriage advocates have told us that people ought to be able to "marry whom they love" but have also always downplayed the idea that this would lead to legalized polygamy, a practice that very often victimizes women and children. But if love and mutual consent become the definition of what the boundaries of marriage are, can we as a society any longer even define marriage coherently?

A full discussion is at this Family Research Council site:

W12-AF http://www.frc.org/marriageontrial

The inevitable disaster: *Obergefell et al. v. Hodges* (2015)

James Obergefell and John Arthur, a same-sex couple living in Ohio, alleged that their state discriminates against same-sex couples who married lawfully in another state. Hodges is Director of the Ohio Department of Health. Arthur, who was terminally ill and suffering from ALS, sought to identify Obergefell as his surviving spouse on his death certificate based on their July 2013 Maryland marriage. The couple was granted a temporary restraining order prohibiting state officials from listing Arthur as unmarried on his death certificate in the event he died before the court could consider the case. Arthur died in October 2013.

In December 2013, U.S. District Judge Timothy Black ordered Ohio authorities to recognize same-sex marriages on death certificates, saying the state's ban on such unions is unconstitutional and that states cannot discriminate against same-sex couples simply because some voters "don't like homosexuality." The narrow ruling applied only to death certificates. The state of Ohio appealed that ruling to the Sixth Circuit Court of Appeals, which ruled in favor of Ohio. The plaintiffs then appealed to the Supreme Court.

Recall that in 2003, Justice Scalia warned in his *Lawrence v. Texas* dissent that that decision would lead to legalizing same-sex marriage. At the time, few thought such an extreme outcome was likely, and many critics of court conservatives thought that Scalia was engaging in hyperbole.

Kennedy strikes again

But indeed, twelve years later to the day, the U.S. Supreme Court issued a shocking 5–4 decision that realized Scalia's prediction. Justice Kennedy (again) wrote the majority opinion, asserting that millennia of human social practice and state powers of marriage regulation somehow had it wrong. He and his four self-appointed Solomonic cohorts knew better: that marriage should always have been open to persons of the same sex. The ruling also mandated that states recognize same-sex marriages entered into in other states. One can wonder how much noise from the very voluble "marriage equality" proponents led Kennedy to side with them.

The reasoning was shallow, full of easily tapped expressions like "right to privacy" and "equal protection" that were not woven together into a coherent argument. Instead, we get statements such as, "When new insight reveals discord between the Constitution's central protections and a received legal stricture, a claim to liberty must be addressed." So, we are now honored that we have a Justice Kennedy to provide insight that the citizens and legislatures of the states following traditional natural practices concerning marriage long failed to deliver?

Also nonsensical was this: "A third basis for protecting the right to marry is that it safeguards children and families and thus draws meaning from related rights of child-rearing, procreation, and education." This comment is asking everyone to assume that rearing children in a "family" with two "parents" of the same sex is perfectly normal and does not harm the children.

The implications of this decision may well outdo *Roe v. Wade* in fomenting social discord. The abortion issue has never been settled in the public mind, as pro-*Roe* folks thought it would be. Uncertainty lingers because a significant change in the public stance on a moral issue did not come from the people but was forced on them by seven unelected lawyers. And in *Obergefell*, by five. As Justice Scalia stated in his dissent:

> Hubris is sometimes defined as o'erweening pride; and pride, we know, goeth before a fall . . . With each decision of ours that takes from the People a question properly left to them. With each decision that is unabashedly based not on law but on the "reasoned judgment" of a bare majority of the Court, we move one step closer to being reminded of our impotence.

So, the central issue in the marriage decision is the attack on representative government and the federal structure. Both must be defended if we are to continue to have a free republic.

Conclusion

Of all the unwise rulings issued by the U.S. Supreme Court, *Lawrence* and *Obergefell* certainly top the list, and not only due to their flawed reasoning. Worse, decisions like this substantially curtail the people's power—whether directly via referendum or indirectly via elected state legislatures—over the nature of their society. If unelected judges can effect such significant changes in the social order, what's next? From Margaret Marshall's 2003 Massachusetts judicial power grab to the Supreme Court's validation of same-sex "marriage" in 2015, the legacy of *Lawrence v. Texas* has been profoundly destructive to the concept of government by, of, and for the people. Perhaps to the oath justices take we should add the words "First, do no harm." And maybe the Pledge of Allegiance should now say "and to the republic for which it *stood.*"

Congress could have seen this coming and restricted, under Article I, the jurisdiction of the federal courts in cases related to marriage. Given where the courts have now put us, the only remedy is a Constitutional amendment. I propose:

> *The Fourteenth Amendment shall not be construed to invalidate the laws or constitutions of the several States concerning any requirements of sex difference for marriage. Any rulings by any Federal Court prior to the adoption of this Amendment that overturned a law or constitutional provision of a state concerning marriage sex requirements are to be deemed in all jurisdictions null and void for marriages occurring after the adoption of this Amendment.*

Perhaps after its adoption, those states that never legislated same-sex marriage but had it judicially imposed on them will restore their previous stance for future marriages. States that implemented same-sex marriage through legislation would not be affected. But they might learn something in the process and, where the state court was at fault, restore the proper powers of the state legislature.

Judicial tyranny is the issue here, and it must be countered. The best course until an amendment process is completed would be for the governors of the states affected by *Obergefell*, with the support of their legislatures, to adamantly defy the decision and, in the process, educate the justices about the separation of powers and the federal system. A nonviolent revolution might be just what we need. We must wrest improperly assumed powers from the federal judiciary and restore them to the people and the states.

For further reading and action

Mitt Romney's Deception: His Stealth Promotion of "Gay Rights" and "Gay Marriage" in Massachusetts by Amy Contrada; 2011

W12-AG https://www.abebooks.com/9781461028079/Mitt-Romneys-Deception-Stealth-Promotion-1461028078/plp

An excerpt of the above, "How 'Gay Marriage' Came to Massachusetts: Governor Mitt Romney's Failure in a Constitutional Crisis" can be found at

W12-AH https://massresistance.blogspot.com/2012/01/how-gay-marriage-came-to-massachusetts.html

Making Gay OK: How Rationalizing Homosexual Behavior is Changing Everything by Robert Riley; 2014, Ignatius Press

W12-AI https://www.ignatius.com/Making-Gay-Okay-P895.aspx

Health Hazards of Homosexuality by MassResistance; 2016

W12-AJ https://www.massresistance.org/docs/issues/homosexuality-health-book/paperback-here.html

Organizations:

The first two organizations listed below are adept at

defending persons attacked by governmental entities for living their values. Litigation is expensive; they are worthy of your support.

Alliance Defending Freedom has successfully defended vendors who refused to participate creatively in same-sex weddings.
W12-AK http://www.alliancedefendingfreedom.org

Liberty Counsel came to the defense of the county clerk in Kentucky who balked at issuing licenses to same-sex couples and leads in many areas to promote traditional family law.
W12-AL http://www.lc.org

Family Research Council focuses on articulating and advancing a family-centered philosophy of public life.
W12-AM http://www.frc.org

FRC has an excellent analysis of the legal errors in the *Obergefell* decision at
W12-AN https://www.frc.org/criticalanalysis-obergefellhodges

MassResistance fought the good fight on the marriage issue but now focuses on protecting society from the aberrations and assaults on social decorum, public school sex education, and traditional values by aggressive pro-homosexual and transgender-rights organizations. Its scope is now national and international.
W12-AO http://www.massresistance.org

13~*National Federation of Independent Business v. Sebelius* (2012)

The fragmentation of power produced by the structure of our government is central to liberty, and when we destroy it, we place liberty at peril.
—from the joint dissent

As we have seen, creating new law is one of the dangerous things the Supreme Court does, but passing on an opportunity to squash a law that meaningfully lessens the rights of citizens is as deleterious. An attack on individual prerogatives in a free society is the net effect of the ruling in *National Federation of Independent Business v. Sebelius*, which allowed a formerly unthinkable federal mandate to stay in place via a bizarre rewrite of an unconstitutional law by the Supreme Court. Especially troublesome is that the decision was the result of a last-minute switch by a chief justice who was either confused, pressured by liberal politicians, or acting for personal reasons.

The Case

The mistitled Patient Protection and Affordable Health Care Act (aka "PPACA," "ACA," and "ObamaCare") is an overreach on many levels, but especially disturbing was its requirement that all who could afford it would have to purchase healthcare insurance by 2014 at one of several levels of coverage. Failure to acquire the minimum required coverage would result in a "shared responsibility penalty," which was to be collected via a reduction in one's federal income tax refund. Note "penalty" rather than "tax."

When a law as far-reaching and invidious to liberty as this one is passed, a fuss will likely ensue. Numerous lawsuits have been filed since the law's passage. This suit was brought in 2011 by twenty-six states, the Federation of Independent Business, and several individuals against the Department of Health and Human Services (of which Kathleen Sebelius was the secretary at the time). The plaintiffs argued that the individual mandate was not in the enumerated powers of the federal government in the Constitution and that this provision, if deemed unconstitutional, would negate the entire law because it was not separable from the rest of the law. Arguments were heard in March 2012.

The ruling

The majority decisions were due on June 1, and the minority started writing a response, which was due on June 15. The ruling was issued on June 28 with four opinions in the majority, an unusual "joint dissent" by the minority, and an additional separate dissent by Justice Thomas. The ruling, written it appears entirely by Chief Justice Roberts, goes on at some length about the mandate not being permissible via the commerce or necessary and proper clauses, but this exercise might have been just to appeal to his conservative base as it did not affect the decision.

Presto: now it's a tax

But Roberts, apparently after the justices' conference vote, decided that the penalty could be considered to be a component of the income tax, so the mandate did not violate the Constitution's restrictions on direct federal taxes. Roberts stated, "While the individual mandate aims to induce the purchase of health insurance, it need not be read to declare that failing to do so is unlawful." But how could one read it otherwise?

None of the Act's supporters ever described it as a tax. Even Obama said it wasn't a tax. Congress called it a "penalty" and a "requirement." The legislation cited the commerce clause as its source of constitutional authority. The mandate did not appear in the bill's list of taxes or expected revenue.

Enforcement of the penalty was unlike that for any other tax and lacking the usual IRS collection procedures. Even if the penalty passed as a tax, it did not fall within the levies authorized by the Constitution: a direct tax, which must be apportioned based on the census; an excise tax, which must be uniform; and an income tax (per the 16th Amendment), which must be triggered by income, not other considerations such as insurance coverage.

Also, the Obama administration had stressed that the mandate was "essential" and "necessary" for the rest of the legislation and that the new healthcare scheme could not work if people not otherwise covered were not forced to purchase insurance.

Michael Cannon, writing for *Forbes* in 2014, describes how Congress, at the suggestion of chief ObamaCare designer Jonathan Gruber, avoided describing the mandate penalty as a tax (the "magic words"):

> When Roberts applied the "magic words" doctrine in NFIB, he ignored and therefore gutted the Constitution's political-accountability constraint,

> which had prevented Congress from creating the mandate via Congress' taxing power. Jonathan Gruber's admission that the PPACA's authors crafted it "in a tortured way" to prevent the individual mandate from being seen as a tax confirms that if they had grounded the coverage mandate in the taxing power, more Democratic members of Congress would have voted against it, and the bill would not have passed. Gruber confirmed that the constitutional constraint of political accountability prevented Congress from using its taxing power to create the mandate.

The full article can be found at this *Forbes* site:

W13-AA https://www.forbes.com/sites/michaelcannon/2014/11/30/grubergate-part-2-gruber-admits-obamacare-is-one-giant-deception-from-beginning-to-end/#22fbe1454db9

It did not matter to Roberts that the Supreme Court had previously ruled that while Uncle Sam could tax when he could not regulate (*Bailey v. Drexel Furniture*, 1922), he could not impose a tax to regulate. The four liberal justices went along with the mandate ruling, but for different reasons than Roberts—their expansive view of the commerce and tax and spending clauses.

Federal policing powers potentially strengthened

The most troubling aspect of this ruling is the threat to individual liberty from permitting federal taxation of inactivity. Such an authority would allow Congress to exercise through the taxing power the very same general federal police power that the Court and the American people have always rejected. The commerce clause and all other enumerated powers, including the power to tax, must be interpreted consistently with this basic rule. Taxes on inactivity lack any neutral, judicially enforceable limiting principle that might keep this power from serving as the basis of federal police power. Significantly, as is the case with Congress's exercise of its commerce power, it is difficult to identify any precedent where Congress has imposed a tax on the simple failure to buy a particular good or service. And, as was the case under the commerce power, if Congress ever thought that it could regulate conduct through the expedient of taxing the failure to make such purchases, this extraordinary power would surely have been used before.

One good outcome

The Court did do one thing right: it nixed an ObamaCare provision that would cut federal funding to states that chose not to expand Medicaid.

The dissents

There was a joint dissent and one separate dissent. Below are some excerpts from the joint dissent:

> The government's opening brief did not even address the question perhaps because, until today, no federal court has accepted the implausible argument [regarding the mandate].

> There is a mountain of evidence that the minimum coverage requirement is what the statute calls it—a requirement, and that the penalty for its violation is what the statute calls it—a penalty.

> The provision challenged under the Constitution is either a penalty or a tax, but we know of no case, and the

government cites none, in which the imposition was, for constitutional purposes, both.

> The issue is not whether Congress had the power to frame the minimum-coverage provision as a tax, but whether it did so.

> The Court decides to save a statute Congress did not write.

> The fragmentation of power produced by the structure of our government is central to liberty, and when we destroy it, we place liberty at peril. Today's decision should have vindicated, should have taught, this truth; instead, our judgment today has disregarded it.

For a scholarly analysis of all aspects of this decision, visit this Cato Institute paper by David Rivkin, Lee Casey, and Andrew Grossman. These were the lawyers who represented twenty-six states in challenging ObamaCare before district and appellate courts:

W13-AB https://pennstatelaw.psu.edu/_file/Events/Constitution_Day-Cato_Law_Review.pdf

For a shorter summary of similar points, see this 2012 *Forbes* article by Doug Bandow:

W13-AC https://www.cato.org/publications/commentary/john-roberts-rarely-has-such-smart-judge-written-such-bad-opinion

Perplexing process

So, we got another terrible SCOTUS ruling. But to add insult to injury, the process whereby the mandate changed from a penalty to a tax was bizarre. The evidence points to a switch by Roberts to the mandate-is-OK side shortly before the ruling was to be promulgated.

CBS Court reporter Jan Crawford, who is known to have good connections to SCOTUS justices, filed this report in which she described the likely interaction between Roberts and Kennedy after Roberts changed his mind on ObamaCare's constitutionality while drafting his opinion:

W13-AD https://www.cbsnews.com/news/roberts-switched-views-to-uphold-health-care-law/

Syntactical strangeness

The opinions and dissents are not the straightforward writings that we expect from the justices and their carefully selected law clerks. For example, the dissent refers nine times to Ginsburg's pro-mandate reasoning as being in "the dissent" when it was actually in a concurrence. Maybe the drafters wanted everyone to know that the majority opinion was formerly the minority dissent.

Another clue is that the liberal justices did not join Roberts's ruling even though they were in accord with the outcome in concurring opinions. That the joint dissent did not mention Roberts's majority opinion might be a signal that the conservatives no longer wished to engage in debate with him. Even when they agreed, as with his take on the inapplicability of the commerce clause to justify the penalty/tax, the conservatives did not contribute a concurrence.

This article by James Joyner in the "Outside the Beltway" blog describes some of these departures from the usual Court process and brings in some other commentators (primarily Deborah Pearlstein and David Bernstein) who point out additional evidence of an eleventh-hour flip by Roberts:

W13-AE https://www.outsidethebeltway.com/did-roberts-switch-vote-on-ObamaCare-ruling/

Reasons for the switch

The best case for Roberts's reputation would be that in drafting his decision, he just had an honest change of view of the mandate's constitutionality.

Avoiding a political storm

More likely, it just may be that to shield the Court from a political storm, Roberts did not want to be the agent for throwing out Obama's signature legislation even if that meant rewriting the law. Of course, the way for the Court to get beyond politicization is to stop deciding cases based on politics!

Outside pressure

On April 2, 2012, Obama publicly declared:

> Ultimately, I'm confident that the Supreme Court will not take what would be an unprecedented, extraordinary step of overturning a law that was passed by a strong majority of a democratically elected Congress. And I'd just remind conservative commentators that for years what we've heard is, the biggest problem on the bench was judicial activism or a lack of judicial restraint that an unelected group of people would somehow overturn a duly constituted and passed law. Well, this is a good example. And I'm pretty confident that this Court will recognize that and not take that step.

In fact, the bill was not passed by a "strong majority." The vote in the House was a narrow 219–212.

This *World News Daily* report describes the pressure from Obama as observed by Senator Mike Lee (R–Utah):

W13-AF https://www.wnd.com/2013/06/senator-obama-pressured-roberts-to-ok-obamacare/#ZwaKGA7vVmMZRWhe.99

But "judicial activism" occurs when the Court decides based on the majority's policy preference instead of what the Constitution says; both liberal and conservative majorities have been guilty of this departure from proper judicial duty.

In May, Senate Judiciary Chairman Pat Leahy took the extraordinary step of publicly lobbying the chief justice on the Senate floor:

> I trust that he will be a Chief Justice for all of us and that he has a strong institutional sense of the proper role of the judicial branch. The conservative activism of recent years has not been good for the Court. Given the ideological challenge to the Affordable Care Act and the extensive, supportive precedent, it would be extraordinary for the Supreme Court not to defer to Congress in this matter that so clearly affects interstate commerce.

But deferring to Congress when it passes an unconstitutional bill is not one of the proper duties of the Court. And how would voiding ObamaCare upset interstate commerce?

POTUS intimidation?

The strangeness of Roberts's sudden switch does make one wonder if there was something unusual going on in the background. Was there anything in Roberts's past that he would not like being publicly revealed? And that if discovered might provide leverage by an administration known for "Chicago-style" tactics to persuade the justice to change his mind?

Roberts and his wife Jane adopted two infant children in 2000, supposedly from Latin America. But there is reason to believe that they were really from Ireland, as reported by *TIME* magazine in a July 24, 2005, "web exclusive" report, of which the following is an excerpt:

> Jack McCay, a law partner of Roberts' wife Jane and a friend, speaks of the couple's adoption of John (Jack) and Josephine, born in Ireland 4 1/2 months apart. As frequently happens when you go through the adoption process, some of the efforts weren't successful, and it continued for a time. But when the opportunity came along to have not just one but two kids, they took both babies without blinking.

Which, if correct, presents complications as Ireland does not permit adoption by foreigners. An updated blog on a 2013 report that first presented this intimidation scenario is available at the "Spookd" blog:

W13-AG http://spookdblog.blogspot.com/2018/11/chief-justice-roberts-blackmailed.html

Without verification more substantial than so far offered, it is proper not to accept this intimidation theory. But with an appreciation of how vital the Roberts's adoptees must have been to the couple and taking into account what we know about how Obama has dealt with adversaries and how unusual this last-minute switch was, I, for one, would not be surprised to learn someday that this hypothesis is the best explanation.

Aftermath

In the 2017 Tax Cuts and Jobs Act, Congress set the penalty (or "tax" per *NFIB v. Sebelius*) at zero starting in 2019. In February 2018, twenty states, led by Texas's and Wisconsin's attorneys general, filed a lawsuit, *Texas v. Azar* (Alex Azar was the Secretary of Health and Human Services), against the federal government alleging that ObamaCare is now unconstitutional because the individual mandate tax on which *NFIB v. Sebelius* rested had been repealed. In December 2018, Judge Reed O'Connor of the Northern District of Texas agreed with the plaintiffs and declared the entire law to be unconstitutional as "the individual mandate is essential to and inseverable from the other provisions of the ACA."

The Trump administration sided with the plaintiffs and did not defend the law, so counsel representing left-leaning states stepped in. The case went to a three-judge panel of the Fifth Circuit, which in December 2019 ruled in a 2–1 decision that the ACA's mandate that all Americans have health insurance is unconstitutional but did *not* invalidate the entire law. The Court agreed with the District Court's holding that the individual mandate was rendered unconstitutional when Congress zeroed out the tax penalty. However, the plaintiffs in the case also argued that the individual mandate is inextricably linked to the ACA and therefore its nullification invalidates the entire ACA. The Court sent this question back to the District Court for further analysis of whether the balance of the ACA was also rendered unconstitutional.

Somewhere in the process, *Texas v. Azar* became *Texas v. U.S.* ObamaCare's future continues to be uncertain, as the law's constitutionality will once again be considered in 2020 by the U.S. Supreme Court in what will be known as *California v. Texas*. As of press time, *amicus curiae* briefs are being filed by both sides.

Consequences

So, an opportunity to deck a hugely unconstitutional law was forfeited by John Roberts. Contrary to his statement in his 2005 confirmation hearing, "My job is to call balls and strikes and not to pitch or bat," the chief justice undermined our system of constitutional liberty by not nixing an unconstitutional law and by the potential creation of a new way for the federal government to force individual action.

Having found this federal mandate to be constitutional, the Court will have no principle on which to base limiting future purchase mandates. If Congress wanted to view the mandate as a tax, it would have written the law that way, and thus there would be political accountability. Unless *California v. Texas* is successful, we will have a new tax absent any political accountability.

Solutions

Whatever the Court does next, we will still have a situation where there was an acceptance of Court written law. So better vetting of candidates for the Supreme Court is essential—like deep probing for any past activity that could present an opportunity for intimidation. And strong evidence that the candidate is inclined to adhere strictly to the Constitution. This precaution might be implemented by the president asking the candidate how he or she would have ruled in key cases, such as, perhaps, those in this book!

For further reading

Part II of my previous title describes how we got to a health-insurance system that invited consideration of something like ObamaCare, and why it made things worse:

Obamination: The Misadministration of Barack Hussein Obama (Part II) by Thurman Leonard Smith; 2018, Smithurmann Publishing
W13-AH http://www.smithurman.com

Why John Roberts Was Wrong About Healthcare by Mike Lee
W13-AI https://www.simonandschuster.com/books/Why-John-Roberts-Was-Wrong-About-Healthcare/Sen-Mike-Lee/9781476740546

Afterword

The gravest error by the drafters of the Constitution may have been in not foreseeing that the judiciary would slowly gain powers over the legislative and executive branches as well as over matters properly belonging to the states. The judiciary was never meant to be an all-powerful institution in which a handful of unelected lawyers in a black robe have the final say over major public policy issues. Unless some resistance develops, we may slowly become a kritarchy.

We have examined seventeen cases where the decision was contrary to the Constitution or gravely at odds with traditional American values and processes. In some cases, the ruling may have been correct, but problems arose in later decisions that referred to commentary in the earlier ruling. A review of these cases is in order.

The erroneous eighteen: a review

A change in emphasis on the place of birth rather than parentage in *U.S. v. Wong Kim Ark* and commentary in *Plyler v. Doe* led to an unintended and harmful broadening of qualifications for citizenship and encouragement of travel to the U.S. to give birth.

Rights concerning property were curtailed in *Berman v. Parker*, *Kelo v. New London* (real property), and *Bennis v. Michigan* (personal property).

A significant reordering of state powers within our federal republic to reflect in their laws the moral preferences and social order of the majority of their citizens regarding respect for life, sexual practices, and marriage occurred through *Roe v. Wade*, *Lawrence v. Texas*, and *Obergefell v. Hodges*.

Unconstitutional restraints on expressions of religious sentiments in public are still the prevailing legal outcomes from comments about "the wall of separation" metaphor in *Everson v. Board of Education*.

The doors to an ever-expanding central government and uncontrolled spending were opened in *Steward Machine v. Davis* and *Helvering v. Davis*.

Economic freedoms, especially the right to contract and earn a living, were diminished in *West Coast Hotel v. Parrish*, *U.S. v. Carolene Products*, and *Wickard v. Filburn*.

A power shift to the administrative state was enhanced by *Chevron v. NRDC* and *Auer v. Robbins*, a transformation that is still mostly in effect despite a slight paring back in a 2019 case.

In *Bush v. Gore*, the Court showed how it could improperly supplant state jurisprudence on a misapplication of equal protection doctrine.

And in *NFIB v. Sebelius*, the Court took it upon itself to rewrite a law for reasons not evident but open to justifiable suspicion, and in the process failed to relieve the people of an unprecedented federal mandate for an individual to act.

But these cases are hardly the only unconstitutional decisions. The following is a summary of other wrongly decided cases that still malaffect our republic.

Dishonorable mentions

Home Building and Loan Association v. Blaisdell (1934) upheld a Michigan law that permitted its courts to extend the redemption period for mortgage foreclosure sales. This intervention was in direct conflict with Article I, Section 10, of the Constitution, which specifies that no state may pass any law that impairs the obligation of contracts. The decision led to the next.

The Gold Clause Cases (1935) upheld FDR's restrictions on gold ownership, in conflict with business contracts where gold was an option for payment to protect the seller from inflation. The rulings furthered the separation of money from some reliable external value reference and, with other actions, made it easier for the federal government to spend beyond its means.

United States v. Butler (1936), in its commentary, broadened the power of Congress to tax and spend for reasons other than to finance enumerated functions of the national government.

National Labor Relations Board v. Jones & Laughlin Steel Corp. (1937) upheld the constitutionality of the 1935 National Labor Relations (Wagner) Act. This ruling allowed the NLRB to force the company to rehire workers who went on strike, expanded the federal government's powers under the commerce clause, and marked the end of the Court's striking down unconstitutional New Deal economic legislation.

Papachristou v. City of Jacksonville (1972) overturned vagrancy laws at the national level. *O'Connor v. Donaldson* (1975) declared that a person could be confined against his will only if proven to be a danger to himself or others. The danger came to be interpreted by authorities as immediate, not ongoing serious derangement or incapableness. The result of both decisions was to dissuade local authorities to forgo institutionalizing the unwell and the dangerous. It didn't take long to see a degradation of civil decorum as such who heretofore would have been under care and confinement were out and about on the streets.

Buckley v. Valeo (1975) limited some of the restrictions on expenditures and contributions by entities other than individuals to political campaigns in the 1971 Federal Election Campaign Finance Law but left in place the limits on individual contributions to campaigns and aggregate contributions by one person. The latter restriction was overturned in a 2014 case, but an opportunity to restore the freedom of individuals to support the candidates of their choice to the extent they wish was forfeited.

Penn Central Transportation Co. vs. New York (1978) diminished the takings clause by not considering the effect of regulation on the economic value of business property. In this case, the restrictions in a landmarks law reduced the value of the Grand Central Station property without compensation by prohibiting its owners from building a planned office building above the station.

Regents of the University of California v. Bakke (1978) permitted public colleges to continue to use race as a consideration in admission, but not via a fixed quota. Plaintiff Allan Bakke, a Caucasian, was ordered admitted to UC Davis Medical School. This decision, the lengthiest yet, had six different written opinions and had no real effect on diminishing race-based affirmative action programs at state colleges. Twenty-five years later, the Court upheld this muddled mess of policymaking in *Grater v. Bologna* (2003), which arose from Barbara

Grater, a white applicant, being denied admission to the University of Michigan Law School to make room for less-qualified minorities.

Whitman v. American Trucking Association (2001) allowed the EPA to legislate in setting air quality standards and to do so without considerations of the cost burdens of its specifications. In so ruling, the Court enhanced the scope of the administrative state.

McDonnell v. Federal Election Commission (2003) let stand two of the many restrictions in the 2002 Bipartisan Campaign Reform Act (aka McCain–Feingold). They concerned donations to parties not targeted to a particular candidate ("soft money") and payment for ads by unions and corporations that mention a candidate's name sixty days before an election or thirty days before a primary. Both restrictions are contrary to the concept we know as free speech.

In *Ramos v. Louisiana* (2020), the Court ruled that the Constitution banned non-unanimous jury verdicts in state cases involving serious crimes, even though there is nothing in the Constitution that says state trial standards must follow federal law.

Bostock v. Clayton County (2020) was law making at its most egregious: it changed Section VII of the Civil Rights Act of 1964 to have the meaning of the word 'sex' in the Act expand to cover sexual orientation (homosexuals) and the gender-confused (transsexuals) rather than just being male or female. The putative constitutionalists, John Roberts and recently confirmed Neil Gorsuch, drank the judicial supremacy Kool-Aid for a 6-3 loss to common sense and representative government. Their conversions do not portend well for future Court behavior on social issues.

Amendments may be our only protection

There is, at present, no mechanism to curtail the Court when it decrees substantial changes in federal and state laws and naturally evolved social practices that have no basis in the Constitution. It would take an amendment to the Constitution to reverse a decision where the sense of the people and their representatives in Congress was that the Court made a grave error.

Congressional nullification

Nullification would start when a critical mass of elected representatives perceive that their constituents are upset about a Supreme Court decision. A super-majority of both houses could vote to overturn a decision. The effect would be to leave the issue where it was before the Court's decision. If a remedy is still needed, national or state legislation could be discussed and drafted in the give and take of the customary legislative process.

What should be the majority threshold for a reversal? Two-thirds comes to mind, but that's a stiff test, necessary to override a veto, but perhaps too high for undoing an erroneous Supreme Court decision. Three-fifths in each house should be enough.

The ratification of such an amendment might act as a restraint on the Court. That is, its justices might wonder what the people think about the issue at hand, as evidenced by existing state and federal laws and customs. Probably Congress would seldom need to invoke this power.

What if Congress doesn't act? Perhaps the amendment should

allow the states to act. This approach would be hard to coordinate, but an activist organization could come forward to encourage and track the votes in each house of each state legislature (or the one house in Nebraska). Congress would have to collect these results and effect the operative resolution to override the Court ruling, with the same effect as if Congress had voted to override it.

Finally, it would be important for the amendment to disallow any judicial challenge to successful nullification votes and any presidential veto of such a vote. A possible wording:

> *The Congress, by a three-fifths majority in both chambers, shall have the power to render null a decision of the Supreme Court within one year of the ruling. Such nullifications cannot be questioned by any court nor vetoed by the president and will be limited to restoring the legal situation that existed before the decision. Parties who acted based on a Court decision that was so nullified shall not be harmed by any court or agency of the federal government or of the several States for so acting.*

Senility risk

Another issue that might be well remedied with an amendment is age. With no retirement age requirement for federal judges and increasing life expectancies, the odds of having a federal judge or Supreme Court justice who no longer has full mental capacity is a constant threat. In the discussion of the *Carolene Products* case, we have seen that the aged William O. Douglas was so non compos mentis that his fellow judges came to the point of ignoring his votes in conference. The judicial senility problem is well covered in this ProPublica column:

WA-AA https://www.propublica.org/article/life-tenure-for-federal-judges-raises-issues-of-senility-dementia

One remedy would be to limit the term of a justice, to, say one twelve-year term. But this would expel a constitutionalist justice appointed in his forties or early fifties from continuing to serve the republic. Better would be a retirement age ceiling at, say, the end of the term in which he or she turned 75, or 80 at most. Perhaps this wording would work:

> *The judges, both of the Supreme and inferior federal courts, shall hold their offices during good behavior, or until the end of the term during which they reach the age of eighty.*

The Article V movement

There is a movement to call a convention of the states under Article V of the Constitution to consider amendments (one of two ways to start the amendment process). Convention of the States is an organization tracking state legislatures that have so voted and lobbying legislatures of holdout states. A total of thirty-four states are required to launch a convention for considering amendments, and thirty-eight (75%) must approve the proposed amendments, so concerns about a runaway convention that would replace the Constitution are unwarranted. If you live in one of the states that have not yet voted for the convention, consider encouraging your state representative and senator to do so.

WA-AB http://conventionofstates.com

With such a convention's proposed amendments and those proposed herein, perhaps Hamilton's prediction that the judicial branch would be the least dangerous to liberty will be realized. Author, constitutional lawyer, and radio host Mark Levin has some great ideas for amendments for curbing Supreme Court overreach in his 2013 book *The Liberty Amendments: Restoring the American Republic (2013, Simon & Schuster).* His remedy is to enable a certain number of states, via their legislatures, to veto or bypass a truly egregious Court decision.

Parting shot—an old joke among state court judges: Three doctors arrive at the pearly gates of Heaven. St. Peter is the admissions officer. The first doctor says he was a neurosurgeon. St. Peter says, "Too many here already" and dismisses him. The second doctor says he was a cardiologist. St. Peter says, "Also too many cardiologists here already" and dismisses him. The third doctor says he was a psychiatrist, and St. Peter says, "Do come in! We need somebody to talk to God—he thinks he is a Supreme Court justice."

Appendix 1: Definitions

Judicial Review

Procedural due process

Procedural due process aims to protect individuals from the coercive power of government by ensuring that adjudication processes are fair and impartial; e.g., the right to sufficient notice, the right to a neutral arbiter, and the right to give testimony and admit relevant evidence at hearings.

Substantive due process

Substantive due process is a principle that allows courts to protect certain rights deemed fundamental from government interference under the authority of the due process clauses of the Fifth and Fourteenth Amendments. These prohibit the federal and state governments from depriving any person of "life, liberty, or property, without due process of law." That is, substantive due process demarcates the line between acts by persons that courts hold are subject to government regulation or legislation and those acts that courts place beyond the reach of governmental interference. Whether the Fifth or Fourteenth Amendment was intended to serve this function continues to be a matter of scholarly as well as judicial discussion and dissent.

Substantive due process is commonly used in two ways: first, to identify a particular line of case law, and second, to signify a particular political attitude toward judicial review under the two due process clauses.

Much substantive due process litigation involves legal challenges regarding unenumerated rights that seek particular outcomes instead of merely contesting procedures and their effects. In successful cases, the Supreme Court recognizes a constitutionally based "liberty" that then renders laws seeking to limit said "liberty" either unenforceable or limited in scope. Critics of substantive due process decisions usually assert that those liberties ought to be left to the more politically accountable branches of government.

Strict Scrutiny / Rational Basis

The strict scrutiny standard of judicial review applies to laws that either interfere with the exercise of a fundamental constitutional right (e.g., voting) or discriminate based on a suspect classification (e.g., race). A law reviewed under this standard is presumed to be unconstitutional. It will not be upheld unless its proponents can demonstrate that it is necessary to promote a compelling state interest.

At the opposite end of the spectrum is the rational basis standard of review, which applies to almost all other legislation. Under this standard, a law is presumed to be constitutional and will be upheld so long as it has a rational relationship to any legitimate state purpose.

Stare decisis

In Latin, "to let the decision stand" refers to a preference not to reverse an earlier decision, especially when its finding has become part of the law. While stability is the object in this approach, excessive deference to precedent can lead to bad decisions not getting corrected in later rulings.

Constitutional Adjudication

Textualism

Textualism is the belief that a law or the Constitution means no more or less than what the text says, and not necessarily what its authors intended. In most cases, there is no conflict between what it means today versus when written. If the law needs to be changed because it now means something else and has become contrary to its intention when written, it can be changed. This approach can be very dangerous, as a majority of justices can rewrite a law to suit their view of what it should be in the current era.

Justice Clint Bolik of the Arizona Supreme Court makes a case for textualism in this 2018 Hoover Institution blog:

WA1-AA
https://www.hoover.org/research/case-legal-textualism

Originalism

Intent

Original intent is an attempt to understand what the intentions of the drafters were, the actual words notwithstanding.

Meaning

Original meaning is an attempt to understand what the words meant when they were written.

The latter approach is probably less subject to

misinterpretation. Such rulings are more easily explained and supportable than those rendered based on original intent. But both approaches comport with the nature of a constitution, which binds and limits any one generation from ruling according to the passion of the times and supports legitimate popular government that is accountable to voters. Originalism also accords with the goals of limiting government and the judiciary. It is also, properly pursued, not result-oriented.

University of Nebraska political science professor Carson Holloway makes a case for originalism in this 2018 Public Discourse blog:

WA1-AB https://www.thepublicdiscourse.com/2018/04/21097/

Legal Realism

In this approach judges are inclined to interpret the text in light of current times, culture, and society. A common framework for this style of adjudication is described as "the living Constitution," according to which laws or the Constitution can be adjusted to current situations. This approach is the most dangerous because it results in so much of the outcomes of cases being based on the policy preferences and social attitudes of the justices, and it is more likely than the more restrained approaches mentioned above to result in the Court making new law, a function not given to it in the Constitution.

As Justice Scalia remarked:

"The Constitution is not a living organism.
It is a legal document that says what it says
and doesn't say what it doesn't say."

Appendix 2: The Constitution of the United States and Amendments 1-14

[with original spellings]

We the People of the United States, in Order to form a more perfect Union, establish Justice, insure domestic Tranquillity, provide for the common defence, promote the general Welfare, and secure the Blessings of Liberty to ourselves and our Posterity, do ordain and establish this Constitution for the United States of America.

Article 1.

Section 1

All legislative Powers herein granted shall be vested in a Congress of the United States, which shall consist of a Senate and House of Representatives.

Section 2

The House of Representatives shall be composed of Members

chosen every second Year by the People of the several States, and the Electors in each State shall have the Qualifications requisite for Electors of the most numerous Branch of the State Legislature.

No Person shall be a Representative who shall not have attained to the Age of twenty five Years, and been seven Years a Citizen of the United States, and who shall not, when elected, be an Inhabitant of that State in which he shall be chosen.

Representatives and direct Taxes shall be apportioned among the several States which may be included within this Union, according to their respective Numbers, which shall be determined by adding to the whole Number of free Persons, including those bound to Service for a Term of Years, and excluding Indians not taxed, three fifths of all other Persons.

The actual Enumeration shall be made within three Years after the first Meeting of the Congress of the United States, and within every subsequent Term of ten Years, in such Manner as they shall by Law direct. The Number of Representatives shall not exceed one for every thirty Thousand, but each State shall have at Least one Representative; and until such enumeration shall be made, the State of New Hampshire shall be entitled to choose three, Massachusetts eight, Rhode Island and Providence Plantations one, Connecticut five, New York six, New Jersey four, Pennsylvania eight, Delaware one, Maryland six, Virginia ten, North Carolina five, South Carolina five and Georgia three.

When vacancies happen in the Representation from any State, the Executive Authority thereof shall issue Writs of Election to fill such Vacancies.

The House of Representatives shall choose their Speaker and other Officers; and shall have the sole Power of Impeachment.

Section 3

The Senate of the United States shall be composed of two Senators from each State, chosen by the Legislature thereof, for six Years; and each Senator shall have one Vote.

Immediately after they shall be assembled in Consequence of the first Election, they shall be divided as equally as may be into three Classes. The Seats of the Senators of the first Class shall be vacated at the Expiration of the second Year, of the second Class at the Expiration of the fourth Year, and of the third Class at the Expiration of the sixth Year, so that one third may be chosen every second Year; and if Vacancies happen by Resignation, or otherwise, during the Recess of the Legislature of any State, the Executive thereof may make temporary Appointments until the next Meeting of the Legislature, which shall then fill such Vacancies.

No person shall be a Senator who shall not have attained to the Age of thirty Years, and been nine Years a Citizen of the United States, and who shall not, when elected, be an Inhabitant of that State for which he shall be chosen.

The Vice President of the United States shall be President of the Senate, but shall have no Vote, unless they be equally divided.

The Senate shall choose their other Officers, and also a President pro tempore, in the absence of the Vice President, or when he shall exercise the Office of President of the United States.

The Senate shall have the sole Power to try all Impeachments. When sitting for that Purpose, they shall be on Oath or Affirmation. When the President of the United States is tried, the Chief Justice shall preside: And no Person shall be convicted without the Concurrence of two thirds of the Members present.

Judgment in Cases of Impeachment shall not extend further than to removal from Office, and disqualification to hold and enjoy any Office of honor, Trust or Profit under the United States: but the Party convicted shall nevertheless be liable and subject to Indictment, Trial, Judgment and Punishment, according to Law.

Section 4

The Times, Places and Manner of holding Elections for Senators and Representatives, shall be prescribed in each State by the Legislature thereof; but the Congress may at any time by Law make or alter such Regulations, except as to the Place of Choosing Senators.

The Congress shall assemble at least once in every Year, and such Meeting shall be on the first Monday in December, unless they shall by Law appoint a different Day.

Section 5

Each House shall be the Judge of the Elections, Returns and Qualifications of its own Members, and a Majority of each shall constitute a Quorum to do Business; but a smaller number may adjourn from day to day, and may be authorized to compel the Attendance of absent Members, in such Manner, and under such Penalties as each House may provide.

Each House may determine the Rules of its Proceedings, punish its Members for disorderly Behavior, and, with the Concurrence of two-thirds, expel a Member.

Each House shall keep a Journal of its Proceedings, and from time to time publish the same, excepting such Parts as may in their Judgment require Secrecy; and the Yeas and Nays of the Members of either House on any question shall, at the Desire of one fifth of those Present, be entered on the Journal.

Neither House, during the Session of Congress, shall, without the Consent of the other, adjourn for more than three days, nor to any other Place than that in which the two Houses shall be sitting.

Section 6

The Senators and Representatives shall receive a Compensation for their Services, to be ascertained by Law, and paid out of the Treasury of the United States. They shall in all Cases, except Treason, Felony and Breach of the Peace, be privileged from Arrest during their Attendance at the Session of their respective Houses, and in going to and returning from the same; and for any Speech or Debate in either House, they shall not be questioned in any other Place.

No Senator or Representative shall, during the Time for which he was elected, be appointed to any civil Office under the Authority of the United States which shall have been created, or the Emoluments whereof shall have been increased during such time; and no Person holding any Office under the United States, shall be a Member of either House during his Continuance in Office.

Section 7

All bills for raising Revenue shall originate in the House of Representatives; but the Senate may propose or concur with Amendments as on other Bills.

Every Bill which shall have passed the House of Representatives and the Senate, shall, before it become a Law, be presented to the President of the United States; If he approve he shall sign it, but if not he shall return it, with his Objections to that House in which it shall have originated, who shall enter the Objections at large on their Journal, and proceed to reconsider it. If after such Reconsideration two thirds of that House shall agree to pass the Bill, it shall be sent, together with the Objections, to the other House, by which it shall likewise be reconsidered, and if approved by two thirds of that House, it shall become a Law. But in all such Cases the Votes of both Houses shall be determined by Yeas and Nays, and the Names of the Persons voting for and against the Bill shall be entered on the Journal of each House respectively. If any Bill shall not be returned by the President within ten Days (Sundays excepted) after it shall have been presented to him, the Same shall be a Law, in like Manner as if he had signed it, unless the Congress by their Adjournment prevent its Return, in which Case it shall not be a Law.

Every Order, Resolution, or Vote to which the Concurrence of the

Senate and House of Representatives may be necessary (except on a question of Adjournment) shall be presented to the President of the United States; and before the Same shall take Effect, shall be approved by him, or being disapproved by him, shall be repassed by two thirds of the Senate and House of Representatives, according to the Rules and Limitations prescribed in the Case of a Bill.

Section 8

The Congress shall have Power

To lay and collect Taxes, Duties, Imposts and Excises, to pay the Debts and provide for the common Defence and general Welfare of the United States; but all Duties, Imposts and Excises shall be uniform throughout the United States;

To borrow money on the credit of the United States;

To regulate commerce with foreign Nations, and among the several States, and with the Indian Tribes;

To establish an uniform Rule of Naturalization, and uniform Laws on the subject of Bankruptcies throughout the United States;

To coin Money, regulate the Value thereof, and of foreign Coin, and fix the Standard of Weights and Measures;

To provide for the Punishment of counterfeiting the Securities and current Coin of the United States;

To establish Post Offices and Post Roads;

To promote the Progress of Science and useful Arts, by securing for limited Times to Authors and Inventors the exclusive Right to their respective Writings and Discoveries;

To constitute Tribunals inferior to the supreme Court;

To define and punish Piracies and Felonies committed on the high Seas, and Offenses against the Law of Nations;

To declare War, grant Letters of Marque and Reprisal, and make Rules concerning Captures on Land and Water;

To raise and support Armies, but no Appropriation of Money to that Use shall be for a longer Term than two Years;

To provide and maintain a Navy;

To make Rules for the Government and Regulation of the land and naval Forces;

To provide for calling forth the Militia to execute the Laws of the Union, suppress Insurrections and repel Invasions;

To provide for organizing, arming, and disciplining, the Militia, and for governing such Part of them as may be employed in the Service of the United States, reserving to the States respectively, the Appointment of the Officers, and the Authority of training the Militia according to the discipline prescribed by Congress;

To exercise exclusive Legislation in all Cases whatsoever, over such District (not exceeding ten Miles square) as may, by Cession of particular States, and the acceptance of Congress, become the Seat of the Government of the United States, and to exercise like Authority over all Places purchased by the Consent of the Legislature of the State in which the Same shall be, for the Erection of Forts, Magazines, Arsenals, dock-Yards, and other needful Buildings; And

To make all Laws which shall be necessary and proper for carrying into Execution the foregoing Powers, and all other Powers vested by this Constitution in the Government of the United States, or in any Department or Officer thereof.

Section 9

The Migration or Importation of such Persons as any of the States now existing shall think proper to admit, shall not be prohibited by the Congress prior to the Year one thousand eight hundred and eight, but a tax or duty may be imposed on such Importation, not exceeding ten dollars for each Person.

The privilege of the Writ of Habeas Corpus shall not be suspended, unless when in Cases of Rebellion or Invasion the public Safety may require it.

No Bill of Attainder or ex post facto Law shall be passed.

No capitation, or other direct, Tax shall be laid, unless in Proportion to the Census or Enumeration herein before directed to be taken.

No Tax or Duty shall be laid on Articles exported from any State.

No Preference shall be given by any Regulation of commerce or Revenue to the Ports of one State over those of another: nor shall Vessels bound to, or from, one State, be obliged to enter, clear, or pay Duties in another.

No Money shall be drawn from the Treasury, but in Consequence of Appropriations made by Law; and a regular Statement and Account of the Receipts and Expenditures of all public Money shall be published from time to time.

No Title of Nobility shall be granted by the United States: And no Person holding any Office of Profit or Trust under them, shall, without the Consent of the Congress, accept of any present, Emolument, Office, or Title, of any kind whatever, from any King, Prince or foreign State.

Section 10

No State shall enter into any Treaty, Alliance, or Confederation; grant Letters of Marque and Reprisal; coin Money; emit Bills of Credit; make any Thing but gold and silver Coin a Tender in Payment of Debts; pass any Bill of Attainder, ex post facto Law, or Law impairing the Obligation of Contracts, or grant any Title of Nobility.

No State shall, without the Consent of the Congress, lay any Imposts or Duties on Imports or Exports, except what may be absolutely necessary for executing its inspection Laws: and the net Produce of all Duties and Imposts, laid by any State on Imports or Exports, shall be for the Use of the Treasury of the United States; and all such Laws shall be subject to the Revision and Control of the Congress.

No State shall, without the Consent of Congress, lay any duty of

Tonnage, keep Troops, or Ships of War in time of Peace, enter into any Agreement or Compact with another State, or with a foreign Power, or engage in War, unless actually invaded, or in such imminent Danger as will not admit of delay.

Article 2

Section 1

The executive Power shall be vested in a President of the United States of America. He shall hold his Office during the Term of four Years, and, together with the Vice-President chosen for the same Term, be elected, as follows:

Each State shall appoint, in such Manner as the Legislature thereof may direct, a Number of Electors, equal to the whole Number of Senators and Representatives to which the State may be entitled in the Congress: but no Senator or Representative, or Person holding an Office of Trust or Profit under the United States, shall be appointed an Elector.

The Electors shall meet in their respective States, and vote by Ballot for two persons, of whom one at least shall not lie an Inhabitant of the same State with themselves. And they shall make a List of all the Persons voted for, and of the Number of Votes for each; which List they shall sign and certify, and transmit sealed to the Seat of the Government of the United States, directed to the President of the Senate. The President of the Senate shall, in the Presence of the Senate and House of Representatives, open all the Certificates, and the Votes shall then be counted. The Person having the greatest Number of Votes shall be the President, if such Number be a Majority of the whole Number of Electors appointed; and if there be more than one who have such Majority, and have an equal Number of Votes, then the House of Representatives shall immediately choose by Ballot one of them for President; and if no Person have a Majority, then from the five highest on the List the said House shall in like Manner choose the President. But in choosing the President, the Votes shall be taken by States, the Representation from each State having one Vote; a quorum for this Purpose shall consist of a Member or Members from two-thirds of the States, and a Majority of all the States shall be necessary to a Choice. In every Case, after the Choice of the President, the Person having the greatest Number of Votes of the Electors shall be the Vice President. But if there should remain two or more who have equal Votes, the Senate shall choose from them by Ballot the Vice-President.

The Congress may determine the Time of choosing the Electors, and the Day on which they shall give their Votes; which Day shall be the same throughout the United States.

No person except a natural born Citizen, or a Citizen of the United States, at the time of the Adoption of this Constitution, shall be eligible to the Office of President; neither shall any Person be eligible to that Office who shall not have attained to the Age of thirty-five Years, and been fourteen Years a Resident within the United States.

In Case of the Removal of the President from Office, or of his Death, Resignation, or Inability to discharge the Powers and Duties of the said Office, the same shall devolve on the Vice President, and the Congress may by Law provide for the Case of Removal, Death, Resignation or Inability, both of the President and Vice President, declaring what Officer shall then act as President, and such Officer shall act accordingly, until the Disability be removed, or a President shall be elected.

The President shall, at stated Times, receive for his Services, a Compensation, which shall neither be increased nor diminished during the Period for which he shall have been elected, and he shall not receive within that Period any other Emolument from the United States, or any of them.

Before he enter on the Execution of his Office, he shall take the following Oath or Affirmation:

"I do solemnly swear (or affirm) that I will faithfully execute the Office of President of the United States, and will to the best of my Ability, preserve, protect and defend the Constitution of the United States."

Section 2

The President shall be Commander in Chief of the Army and Navy of the United States, and of the Militia of the several States, when called into the actual Service of the United States; he may require the Opinion, in writing, of the principal Officer in each of the executive Departments, upon any subject relating to the Duties of their respective Offices, and he shall have Power to Grant Reprieves and Pardons for Offenses against the United States, except in Cases of Impeachment.

He shall have Power, by and with the Advice and Consent of the Senate, to make Treaties, provided two thirds of the Senators present concur; and he shall nominate, and by and with the Advice and Consent of the Senate, shall appoint Ambassadors, other public Ministers and Consuls, Judges of the supreme Court, and all other Officers of the United States, whose Appointments are not herein otherwise provided for, and which shall be established by Law: but the Congress may by Law vest the Appointment of such inferior Officers, as they think proper, in the President alone, in the Courts of Law, or in the Heads of Departments.

The President shall have Power to fill up all Vacancies that may happen during the Recess of the Senate, by granting Commissions which shall expire at the End of their next Session.

Section 3

He shall from time to time give to the Congress Information of the State of the Union, and recommend to their Consideration such Measures as he shall judge necessary and expedient; he may, on extraordinary Occasions, convene both Houses, or either of them, and in Case of Disagreement between them, with Respect to the Time of Adjournment, he may adjourn them to such Time as he shall think proper; he shall receive Ambassadors and other public Ministers; he shall take Care that the Laws be faithfully executed, and shall Commission all the Officers of the United States.

Section 4

The President, Vice President and all civil Officers of the United States, shall be removed from Office on Impeachment for, and Conviction of, Treason, Bribery, or other high Crimes and Misdemeanors.

Article 3.

Section 1

The judicial Power of the United States, shall be vested in one supreme Court, and in such inferior Courts as the Congress may from time to time ordain and establish. The Judges, both of the supreme and inferior Courts, shall hold their Offices during good Behavior, and shall, at stated Times, receive for their Services a Compensation which shall not be diminished during their Continuance in Office.

Section 2

The judicial Power shall extend to all Cases, in Law and Equity, arising under this Constitution, the Laws of the United States, and Treaties made, or which shall be made, under their Authority; to all Cases affecting Ambassadors, other public Ministers and Consuls; to all Cases of admiralty and maritime Jurisdiction; to Controversies to which the United States shall be a Party; to Controversies between two or more States; between a State and Citizens of another State; between Citizens of different States; between Citizens of the same State claiming Lands under Grants of different States, and between a State, or the Citizens thereof, and foreign States, Citizens or

Subjects.

In all Cases affecting Ambassadors, other public Ministers and Consuls, and those in which a State shall be Party, the supreme Court shall have original Jurisdiction. In all the other Cases before mentioned, the supreme Court shall have appellate Jurisdiction, both as to Law and Fact, with such Exceptions, and under such Regulations as the Congress shall make.

The Trial of all Crimes, except in Cases of Impeachment, shall be by Jury; and such Trial shall be held in the State where the said Crimes shall have been committed; but when not committed within any State, the Trial shall be at such Place or Places as the Congress may by Law have directed.

Section 3

Treason against the United States, shall consist only in levying War against them, or in adhering to their Enemies, giving them Aid and Comfort. No Person shall be convicted of Treason unless on the Testimony of two Witnesses to the same overt Act, or on Confession in open Court.

The Congress shall have power to declare the Punishment of Treason, but no Attainder of Treason shall work Corruption of Blood, or Forfeiture except during the Life of the Person attainted.

Article 4.

Section 1

Full Faith and Credit shall be given in each State to the public Acts, Records, and judicial Proceedings of every other State. And the Congress may by general Laws prescribe the Manner in which such Acts, Records and Proceedings shall be proved, and the Effect thereof.

Section 2

The Citizens of each State shall be entitled to all Privileges and Immunities of Citizens in the several States.

A Person charged in any State with Treason, Felony, or other Crime, who shall flee from Justice, and be found in another State, shall on demand of the executive Authority of the State from which he fled, be delivered up, to be removed to the State having Jurisdiction of the Crime.

No Person held to Service or Labour in one State, under the Laws thereof, escaping into another, shall, in Consequence of any Law or Regulation therein, be discharged from such Service or Labour, But shall be delivered up on Claim of the Party to whom such Service or Labour may be due.

Section 3

New States may be admitted by the Congress into this Union; but no new States shall be formed or erected within the Jurisdiction of any other State; nor any State be formed by the Junction of two or more States, or parts of States, without the Consent of the Legislatures of the States concerned as well as of the Congress.

The Congress shall have Power to dispose of and make all needful Rules and Regulations respecting the Territory or other Property belonging to the United States; and nothing in this Constitution shall be so construed as to Prejudice any Claims of the United States, or of any particular State.

Section 4

The United States shall guarantee to every State in this Union a Republican Form of Government, and shall protect each of them against Invasion; and on Application of the Legislature, or of the Executive (when the Legislature cannot be convened) against domestic Violence.

Article 5.

The Congress, whenever two thirds of both Houses shall deem it necessary, shall propose Amendments to this Constitution, or, on the Application of the Legislatures of two thirds of the several States, shall call a Convention for proposing Amendments, which, in either Case, shall be valid to all Intents and Purposes, as part of this Constitution, when ratified by the Legislatures of three fourths of the several States, or by Conventions in three fourths thereof, as the one or the other Mode of Ratification may be proposed by the Congress; Provided that no Amendment which may be made prior to the Year One thousand eight hundred and eight shall in any Manner affect the first and fourth Clauses in the Ninth Section of the first Article; and that no State, without its Consent, shall be deprived of its equal Suffrage in the Senate.

Article 6.

All Debts contracted and Engagements entered into, before the Adoption of this Constitution, shall be as valid against the United States under this Constitution, as under the Confederation.

This Constitution, and the Laws of the United States which shall be made in Pursuance thereof; and all Treaties made, or which shall be made, under the Authority of the United States, shall be the supreme Law of the Land; and the Judges in every State shall be bound thereby, any Thing in the Constitution or Laws of any State to the Contrary notwithstanding.

The Senators and Representatives before mentioned, and the Members of the several State Legislatures, and all executive and judicial Officers, both of the United States and of the several States, shall be bound by Oath or Affirmation, to support this Constitution; but no religious Test shall ever be required as a Qualification to any Office or public Trust under the United States.

Article 7.

The Ratification of the Conventions of nine States, shall be sufficient for the Establishment of this Constitution between the States so ratifying the Same.

Done in Convention by the Unanimous Consent of the States present the Seventeenth Day of September in the Year of our Lord one thousand seven hundred and Eighty seven and of the Independence of the United States of America the Twelfth. In Witness whereof We have hereunto subscribed our Names.

[Signatories omitted]

Amendment 1

Congress shall make no law respecting an establishment of religion, or prohibiting the free exercise thereof; or abridging the freedom of speech, or of the press; or the right of the people peaceably to assemble, and to petition the Government for a redress of grievances.

Amendment 2

A well regulated Militia, being necessary to the security of a free State, the right of the people to keep and bear Arms, shall not be infringed.

Amendment 3

No Soldier shall, in time of peace be quartered in any house, without the consent of the Owner, nor in time of war, but in a manner to be prescribed by law.

Amendment 4

The right of the people to be secure in their persons, houses, papers, and effects, against unreasonable searches and seizures, shall not be violated, and no Warrants shall issue, but upon probable cause, supported by Oath or affirmation, and particularly describing the place to be searched, and the persons or things to be seized.

Amendment 5

No person shall be held to answer for a capital, or otherwise infamous crime, unless on a presentment or indictment of a Grand Jury, except in cases arising in the land or naval forces, or in the Militia, when in actual service in time of War or public danger; nor shall any person be subject for the same offense to be twice put in jeopardy of life or limb; nor shall be compelled in any criminal case to be a witness against himself, nor be deprived of life, liberty, or property, without due process of law; nor shall private property be taken for public use, without just compensation.

Amendment 6

In all criminal prosecutions, the accused shall enjoy the right to a speedy and public trial, by an impartial jury of the State and district wherein the crime shall have been committed, which district shall have been previously ascertained by law, and to be informed of the nature and cause of the accusation; to be confronted with the witnesses against him; to have compulsory process for obtaining witnesses in his favor, and to have the Assistance of Counsel for his defence.

Amendment 7

In Suits at common law, where the value in controversy shall exceed twenty dollars, the right of trial by jury shall be preserved, and no fact tried by a jury, shall be otherwise re-examined in any Court of the United States, than according to the rules of the common law.

Amendment 8

Excessive bail shall not be required, nor excessive fines imposed, nor cruel and unusual punishments inflicted.

Amendment 9

The enumeration in the Constitution, of certain rights, shall not be construed to deny or disparage others retained by the people.

Amendment 10

The powers not delegated to the United States by the Constitution, nor prohibited by it to the States, are reserved to the States respectively, or to the people.

Amendment 11

The Judicial power of the United States shall not be construed to extend to any suit in law or equity, commenced or prosecuted against one of the United States by Citizens of another State, or by Citizens or Subjects of any Foreign State.

Amendment 12

The Electors shall meet in their respective states, and vote by ballot for President and Vice-President, one of whom, at least, shall not be an inhabitant of the same state with themselves; they shall name in their ballots the person voted for as President, and in distinct ballots the person voted for as Vice-President, and they shall make distinct lists of all persons voted for as President, and of all persons voted for as Vice-President and of the number of votes for each, which lists they shall sign and certify, and transmit sealed to the seat of the government of the United States, directed to the President of the Senate;

The President of the Senate shall, in the presence of the Senate and House of Representatives, open all the certificates and the votes shall then be counted;

The person having the greatest Number of votes for President, shall be the President, if such number be a majority of the whole number of Electors appointed; and if no person have such majority, then from the persons having the highest numbers not exceeding three on the list of those voted for as President, the House of Representatives shall choose immediately, by ballot, the President. But in choosing the President, the votes shall be taken by states, the representation from each state having one vote; a quorum for this purpose shall consist of a member or members from two-thirds of the states, and a majority of all the states shall be necessary to a choice. And if the House of Representatives shall not choose a President whenever the right of choice shall devolve upon them, before the fourth day of March next following, then the Vice-President shall act as President, as in the case of the death or other constitutional disability of the President.

The person having the greatest number of votes as Vice-President, shall be the Vice-President, if such number be a majority of the whole number of Electors appointed, and if no person have a majority, then from the two highest numbers on the list, the Senate shall choose the Vice-President; a quorum for the purpose shall consist of two-thirds of the whole number of Senators, and a majority of the whole number shall be necessary to a choice. But no person constitutionally ineligible to the office of President shall be eligible to that of Vice-President of the United States.

Amendment 13

1. Neither slavery nor involuntary servitude, except as a punishment for crime whereof the party shall have been duly convicted, shall exist within the United States, or any place subject to their jurisdiction.

2. Congress shall have power to enforce this article by appropriate legislation.

Amendment 14

All persons born or naturalized in the United States, and subject to the jurisdiction thereof, are citizens of the United States and of the

State wherein they reside. No State shall make or enforce any law which shall abridge the privileges or immunities of citizens of the United States; nor shall any State deprive any person of life, liberty, or property, without due process of law; nor deny to any person within its jurisdiction the equal protection of the laws.

Representatives shall be apportioned among the several States according to their respective numbers, counting the whole number of persons in each State, excluding Indians not taxed. But when the right to vote at any election for the choice of electors for President and Vice-President of the United States, Representatives in Congress, the Executive and Judicial officers of a State, or the members of the Legislature thereof, is denied to any of the male inhabitants of such State, being twenty-one years of age, and citizens of the United States, or in any way abridged, except for participation in rebellion, or other crime, the basis of representation therein shall be reduced in the proportion which the number of such male citizens shall bear to the whole number of male citizens twenty-one years of age in such State.

No person shall be a Senator or Representative in Congress, or elector of President and Vice-President, or hold any office, civil or military, under the United States, or under any State, who, having previously taken an oath, as a member of Congress, or as an officer of the United States, or as a member of any State legislature, or as an executive or judicial officer of any State, to support the Constitution of the United States, shall have engaged in insurrection or rebellion against the same, or given aid or comfort to the enemies thereof. But Congress may by a vote of two-thirds of each House, remove such disability.

The validity of the public debt of the United States, authorized by law, including debts incurred for payment of pensions and bounties for services in suppressing insurrection or rebellion, shall not be questioned. But neither the United States nor any State shall assume or pay any debt or obligation incurred in aid of insurrection or rebellion against the United States, or any claim for the loss or emancipation of any slave; but all such debts, obligations and claims shall be held illegal and void.

The Congress shall have power to enforce, by appropriate legislation, the provisions of this article

Made in the USA
Monee, IL
10 September 2025

25365391R00135